RESONATE

with

STILLNESS

RESONATE

with

STILLNESS

Daily Contemplations

From the words of
Swami Muktānanda
Gurumayi Chidvilāsānanda

SIDDHA YOGA®

A SIDDHA YOGA PUBLICATION
PUBLISHED BY SYDA FOUNDATION®
www.siddhayoga.org

Published by SYDA Foundation
PO Box 600, 371 Brickman Road, South Fallsburg, NY 12779-0600, USA

Photograph on the front cover: The Yajña Maṇḍap, located in Gurudev Siddha Peeṭh, the first Siddha Yoga Ashram in India.

Acknowledgments

PRODUCTION EDITOR: Pamela Williams
DESIGNER: Cheryl Crawford
EDITOR: Kshama Jane Ferrar
TYPESETTER: Victoria Light
PRINT COORDINATOR: Francois Simon
TRANSLATION COORDINATOR: Vera Mezina

Original Language: English and Hindi

Printed in the United States of America

First published 1995
20 19 18 17 16 15 14 13   3 4 5 6 7 8 9 10

Library of Congress has catalogued the original edition as follows:
Muktananda, Swami, 1908–
    Resonate with stillness : daily contemplations / from the words of Swami Muktananda, Swami Chidvilasananda.
        p.   cm.
    "A Siddha Yoga publication."
    ISBN 0-911307-42-7 (pbk.)
    1. Hindu meditations. 2. Hindu devotional calendars.
I. Chidvilasananda, Gurumayi. II. Title.
BL1146.M77R46   1995
294.5'43—dc20   95-41463
                                                            CIP

About the SYDA Foundation

The SYDA Foundation is a not-for-profit organization that protects, preserves, and facilitates the dissemination of the Siddha Yoga teachings. The SYDA Foundation also guides the philanthropic expressions of the Siddha Yoga path. These include The PRASAD Project, which provides health, education, and sustainable development programs for children, families, and communities in need; and the Muktabodha Indological Research Institute, which contributes to the preservation of the scriptural heritage of India.

Notes on the Text

The teachings in this volume are selections from the spoken and written words of Gurumayi Chidvilāsānanda, the Guru of the Siddha Yoga path, and her Guru, Swami Muktānanda (1908–1982). These daily teachings focus on twelve fundamental themes of Siddha Yoga philosophy and culture—one theme for each month of the year.

Throughout the text, terms in languages other than English are printed in italics; all proper names are printed in roman type. The standard international transliteration conventions for Sanskrit and modern South Asian languages have been employed. For the reader's convenience a Sanskrit pronunciation guide follows the text.

CONTENTS

❧

The Siddha Yoga Path

Guide to Sanskrit Pronunciation

Glossary

Further Reading

The Siddha Yoga Path

SIDDHA YOGA is a spiritual path of teachings and practices imparted by the Siddha Yoga Gurus: Gurumayi Chidvilāsānanda and Swami Muktānanda (1908–1982).

GURUMAYI CHIDVILĀSĀNANDA is the spiritual head of the Siddha Yoga path. Gurumayi is a Siddha Guru, an enlightened meditation Master who has the rare power to awaken within a human being the inner spiritual energy known as Kuṇḍalinī Śakti. Seekers around the world have received this sacred initiation, *śaktipāt dīkṣā*, from Gurumayi and, with her guidance, progress toward the highest spiritual attainment—the unwavering experience of divinity within themselves and all of creation.

Gurumayi received the divine power and authority of the Guru of the Siddha Yoga path from her Guru, Swami Muktānanda, in 1982.

SWAMI MUKTĀNANDA, affectionately known by his students as Bābā, received *śaktipāt dīkṣā* in 1947 from his Guru, Bhagavān Nityānanda. In 1961, Bhagavān Nityānanda transmitted to Bābā Muktānanda the power and authority to bestow *śaktipāt* initiation.

Over the years, Bābā gave form and articulation to the Siddha Yoga path, bringing together the teachings that he received from his Guru, the spiritual knowledge and practices from the timeless wisdom of India, and his own direct experience. In the course of three world tours between 1970 and 1982, Bābā gave the Siddha Yoga teachings and practices to seekers around the globe.

BHAGAVĀN NITYĀNANDA, also known as Baḍe Bābā, was a *śaktipāt* Guru and a saint widely revered throughout India. He came to settle in the village of Gaṇeśpurī in Mahārāṣtra state. It was here, in the mid-1940s, that Swami Muktānanda became a disciple of Bhagavān Nityānanda. In 1956, Bhagavān Nityānanda asked Swami Muktānanda to establish his own Ashram less than a mile from Gaṇeśpurī. This became the Siddha Yoga Ashram known as Gurudev Siddha Peeth.

RESONATE
with
STILLNESS

JANUARY

Honor Your Self

JANUARY

1

*E*very new beginning is beautiful, filled with extraordinary opportunities, like a door opening on a whole new life. In beginnings there is a childlike innocence, and this innocence is filled with humility, filled with patience. On the spiritual path, these two virtues are paramount: humility and patience. To a beginner they are readily available.

A beginner knows he doesn't know, so there is humility. A beginner knows for certain something is going to happen, so there is patience. With humility and patience as his support, a beginner advances into the unknown to discover a glorious event that is yet to occur.

Even after achieving the goal of all spiritual practices, you cannot be indifferent to a new beginning. A beginning is forever full of magic, enchantment, and treasures to be explored. No matter what the occasion, a new beginning must be approached with a mystical awareness of its potential.

Gurumayi Chidvilāsānanda

*R*enounce old habits so the new path can be illumined. Be prepared to let go of old sorrows and welcome a new beginning with an open heart — no concepts and no limitations.

If you're still hanging on to the old year, let it go back into its Source. We're ready for something new! Let yourself breathe in the newness, the freshness, the fragrance of the new year.

The new year contains everything you've ever wanted: God's love.

Gurumayi Chidvilāsānanda

*H*uman life is sublime. It is mysterious and worth knowing. It is the blossoming flower of happiness, the flame of God. But only to a person who really lives does life reveal its mystery. Life is great only for a person who is truly alive. What does it mean to be truly alive?

To be truly alive means to know your own Self, to know the Consciousness that pervades everywhere in the universe and lives in the human heart.

Swami Muktānanda

If you were to see yourself through meditation, you would find that you are worthy of great honor.

If you were to see yourself as you really are, you would realize that you are neither man nor woman; you don't belong to any religion or race or caste or creed. You are really and truly the most fascinating, beautiful light of God. The highest Truth exists within your heart.

Swami Muktānanda

*B*ābā Muktānanda's message was very simple. He said:

Honor your own Self.
Meditate on your own Self.
Worship your own Self.
Kneel to your own Self.
Understand your own Self.
Your God dwells within you as you.

Right in the beginning one should understand this Self is not the body, this Self is not the ego. Meditation on the Self is meditation on the depth of the soul, on the great Self that is pure, that is love, that is filled with bliss.

Even if you haven't had the experience of this great Self, just by hearing that it exists within, you can actually feel the layers of ignorance falling away; you can feel the wisdom sprouting within.

It's always amazing how a Master can do this: he tells you something very simple, and the heavens open wide.

Gurumayi Chidvilāsānanda

In all the changes in one's life, there is something that never, never changes — whether you are a child or an elderly person, whether you're awake or in deep sleep. A beam of light supports everything — that which is straight and that which is crooked. It is called the inexhaustible flow of Consciousness. It is ever-present, giving each one the awareness, "I exist."

Gurumayi Chidvilāsānanda

*J*ust as on the earth gravity holds everything down, in the same way on a higher scale, it is the supreme Self that is the magnetic pull toward the core of being. A true seeker is always searching for this great power. It is this power that makes him think, speak, and perform all his actions. So he wants to know, "What is this great power?" A true seeker longs to know the power that is hidden in beauty, in stagnant water, in a shooting star, and also in a harsh word. He wants to know the power hidden in boredom, the power that exists in pain and suffering, in a river, in hatred, or in the call of a bird. A true seeker wants to know, "What is this great power that exists in all things?" It exists in a person who is bad; it exists in a person who is good. It exists in a nice house, also in a dilapidated house. It exists in a person who is very humble, also in a person who is very egocentric. What is this great power?

The *Chāndogya Upaniṣad* says:

> *That is the soul, free from evil, ageless,*
> *deathless, sorrowless, hungerless, thirstless,*
> *whose desire is the Real,*
> *whose essence is the Real.*

Gurumayi Chidvilāsānanda

To forget your own Self and consider yourself something else —
this is ignorance. When algae spread over the surface of water,
they cover the water so that you cannot see it. When clouds form
in the sky, they cover the sky so that you cannot see it. When
cataracts cover the pupils of the eyes, they block your vision. In
the same way, the ego acts as a screen, as a veil, which hides the
divinity of your own Self.

As long as you do not know your true nature, you are a mere *jīva*,
a small individual. You are a victim of death. You constantly drink
the juice of jealousy, pride, and anger. But once you understand
your Self, then you drink nectar — the nectar of the Self, the
nectar of supreme bliss. As you turn within and your inner Śakti,
your inner divine force, is awakened, you cease to be a *jīva*, an
individual. You become Śiva, the Lord himself.

Swami Muktānanda

The supreme Being, who is the supreme radiance, is beyond
all darkness. Look at the sun in the sky; it can be covered by
clouds, it can be hidden by trees, it can be concealed by
mountains, it can be eclipsed by the moon. However, there is
a greater sun within, which can never be covered by anything.
It continually blazes, it continually burns inside. This is why,
no matter how shrouded we are by illusion, there comes a
point in our lives when we feel, "I want to know the Truth,
I want to know God, I want to know something beyond
the life that I have grown accustomed to."

You have this yearning because the great sun is continually
blazing inside, burning away the mist of illusion.

Gurumayi Chidvilāsānanda

*G*od is the Self.
He is the light of knowledge.
He is blazing.
He is shimmering.
He is scintillating.
He is vibrating in your heart.
He is sitting right there
within you.

Swami Muktānanda

JANUARY

11

For the experience of the great energy, the great Self,
you must turn your gaze inward. That which you are
looking for is beckoning to you from within.

Gurumayi Chidvilāsānanda

*J*ust as everything precious is hidden,
God, so precious, is also hidden
within your own being.

Gurumayi Chidvilāsānanda

JANUARY

13

*A*fter one has fully realized one's Self, one discovers that the most valuable thing in life is to love others. We should honor each other because all of us have come from the same God; we should respect each other as divine. You don't have to engage in any spectacular project. What is important is to look upon everyone with a deep sense of honor, because your own heart and mind are influenced by the way you look at others. If you could do just that, you would be rendering the greatest service to your fellow beings; and the reward of that service would be inner peace and God-realization. Looking upon others as embodiments of supreme Truth is the highest religion, the highest worship, and the highest form of charity.

For as many moments as you are able to look upon others as divine, as manifestations of God, during those same moments you will experience a most amazing inner bliss.

Swami Muktānanda

JANUARY

14

*W*hen Self-recognition takes place, reunion within also takes place. It is this reunion that gives rise to incredible ecstasy, incredible love. Then your old pettiness just falls away, and you become a shelter of supreme compassion. Every object you touch vibrates with your compassion. Every person you see is affected by your compassion. Your dwelling place grows lush with compassion.

This Self-recognition is a dynamic event, an explosion that shatters any and all mind-born, limited, selfish identities.

Gurumayi Chidvilāsānanda

JANUARY

15

*T*he sages have told us:

Know the One in your own heart, and then you will understand the heart of each person.

Know the One in your own mind; then you will recognize that One in each person's mind.

Know the One in your own life; then you will experience that One in everyone else's life.

When you recognize divinity within yourself, then that is what you long to see in others; and due to that longing, that is what you are able to see in everyone else.

Gurumayi Chidvilāsānanda

JANUARY

16

*W*ithin every human being there is a divine effulgence —
the *nīla-bindu*, the Blue Pearl, which everyone should see at least
once. After you have seen it, you become steady and tranquil.
Our outward beauty and our spiritual beauty derive from its
existence. When it leaves us, we are carried away to a cemetery.

Because of this light, we are able to love one another. There is so
much love in this light. It contains no maleness, no femaleness,
for it is the same in both men and women. There is no East or
West in it either, no Christianity, no Hinduism, no Islam. That
light is pure blue Consciousness. No religion, faith, or race
can reach it. It is the God who transcends all religions, and it
is intensely beautiful. When you see it in meditation, you are
speechless. Whatever we do is done simply to see it. After I
saw the blue inner light, I was cured of my religious, racial,
and national beliefs because I could see the same light in others
too, and I could see that all these religious and racial distinctions
were artificial. In that light they don't exist.

When, through the grace of Nityānanda Bābā, I saw the light of
pure Consciousness, it settled in my eyes and transformed them.

Swami Muktānanda

JANUARY

17

In each one of us, there is a place of perfect silence. It is there, whether we know it or not, like the void within a grain of salt or within an elephant or even within the ether. Supreme silence resides at our core in the same way.

This silence is not dead. It vibrates. You can find it on the stony peaks of high mountains where the stillness echoes, or at the bottom of deep, empty wells in the deafening quiet.

In the same way, within every one of us there is a deep silence, and it has a pulse. It is the force of this silence that drives a seeker to go within so that he can become established in his true nature, so that he can have the constant experience, "I am."

Gurumayi Chidvilāsānanda

JANUARY

18

*O*nce you experience the inner silence, you never feel empty,
because in the inner silence you can hear the stars speak,
you can hear the voice of the water, you can hear the voice
of the great Self. You can hear and you understand.

Gurumayi Chidvilāsānanda

JANUARY

19

*T*he supreme Self, the still center of your own being, holds
you together when everything else is falling apart. Good and bad
swirl around it like children swinging around a maypole, but the
center holds fast. Unmoving and untouched, the supreme Self is
totally unaffected by your ups and downs. It is eternally blissful
and absolutely pure.

Gurumayi Chidvilāsānanda

JANUARY

20

*T*he Self is the most subtle of all subtle things. It is highly
secret and mysterious, and it has no name, no color, and
no form. Even though it is without attributes, the sages
have described its nature as *sac-cid-ānanda* — existence,
Consciousness, and bliss absolute.

Sat means absolute Truth, the Truth that exists in all places,
in all things, and at all times. If that were not omnipresent, it
would not be the Truth; it would not have absolute existence.
For instance, a chair that exists in New York does not exist in
Los Angeles. It exists now, but it did not exist last year. So
that chair does not have absolute existence. But the Self
exists in the east, in the west, in the north, and in the south.
It exists in all countries. It is here today, it was here yesterday,
and it will be here tomorrow. The Self is not bound by any
place, thing, or time.

God, the Self, exists everywhere in his fullness. Being present
in everything, he is also present within us.

Swami Muktānanda

The Self is *cit*, Consciousness, that which illumines everything. *Cit* makes us aware of all outer objects as well as of our inner feelings. When we are upset or unhappy, Consciousness illumines these feelings, and when we feel bliss, Consciousness makes us aware of that, too. It makes us aware that God exists inside, and if we think that God does not exist because we have not seen him, it is *cit* that gives rise to this understanding as well. *Cit* illumines the Reality that exists in all places, all things, and all times.

The Self is *cit*, and it illumines itself as well as everything else.

Swami Muktānanda

*T*he Self is *ānanda*, bliss, and it can be understood only after we attain That.

This bliss, *ānanda*, is far greater than the bliss that arises from seeing a beautiful form, hearing a melodious sound, tasting delicious food, or experiencing the softness of a touch. The pleasures born of the senses depend on the senses, and if the objects of pleasure disappear, the bliss also disappears. But the bliss of the Self does not depend on any external factor. It is completely independent; it arises, unconditioned, from within. Even when the mind and the intellect come close to the Self, they are unable to experience that bliss fully. The great being Jñāneśvar Mahārāj said, "The effulgence of the Self is ever-new." The bliss of the Self constantly renews itself.

Swami Muktānanda

JANUARY

23

As I was wandering around India, sometimes I would come across great beings who laughed constantly, and I would wonder, "Don't they ever get tired of laughing?" Now I understand why they were always laughing. They would feel bliss and laugh, and in the next moment they would feel a new kind of bliss, so they would laugh again. Because their bliss was ever-new, they would keep laughing and laughing.

One who depends on the senses for happiness is constantly looking for new things to satisfy him. He has to have new tastes, new music, new love. But since the bliss of the Self is always different, a yogi never gets tired of it.

Swami Muktānanda

The knowers of the Truth experience God in this human body, so they consider this body sacred. They say, "The body is the temple of God."

What is a temple? It is the place where you have installed your chosen deity, where the image of a saint exists. It's where you let devotion burn brightly. It's where you stand still, seeking refuge from the worries of the world. It's where you go to experience the deep, ever-existing bond of peace between you and your Beloved. And a temple is a wish-fulfilling tree. A temple is a place where God can be seen. So when they say, "The body is a temple of God," the phrase makes you stop in your tracks and reevaluate the way you've been treating your body.

The glory of the human body is that it contains the experience of God.

Gurumayi Chidvilāsānanda

If a person takes birth in this human body
and leaves this world
without knowing the inner Self,
then what is great about him?
Even a dog lives,
even a monkey lives,
even a tree lives.
Go everywhere,
do everything,
meet everyone,
love everyone,
but never forget your Self.
Never think that anything exists
other than your Self.
There is nothing but you,
nothing different from you,
nothing to attain other than you,
nothing that can be taken from you.
That is all you need to understand.
There is nothing to know other than that.

Swami Muktānanda

There is no temple other than
the human body.
There is no God other than
the inner Self.

Swami Muktānanda

JANUARY

27

There isn't a single moment in our lives when God disappears. There isn't a single moment in our lives when our heart closes. The heart is constantly experiencing the presence of God. There may be a moment when you forget to see God, when you forget to visit your own heart, but there is never a moment when God disappears, never a moment when your heart closes.

Remember this: God's love is unconditional; your heart is always open.

Gurumayi Chidvilāsānanda

ove your own self, love your own body, love your own face,
love your own mind, love your own inner Self. Honor yourself.

Sit in a solitary corner and look at yourself. Say to your body,
"How beautiful this body is; it is endowed with such wonderful
capabilities. It has eyes that can see things in such a beautiful
manner. God himself dwells in it. The in-breath and out-breath
flow in it. It has a mind that can think. It is the seat of bliss and
gladness. How blessed I am. What more could I need? Is there
anything that I could want when I have such a perfect system?"

This is the best kind of love.

Swami Muktānanda

See your own body not as a mere physical body, but as the house of God. When you do that, the great experience wants to reveal itself to you. And the moment you touch your own Self, it's as if a piece of wood has been touched by fire. Everything is lit up with that flame.

Give it a wonderful try. Don't give up. Do it! In this house of God, find that love and experience it.

Gurumayi Chidvilāsānanda

JANUARY

30

Don't attach any importance to feelings of unworthiness. You are not your feelings; you are the place where feelings arise. Just as in the upper spaces clouds appear and vanish, in the space of the heart endless feelings and thoughts rise and set. Why should you attach any special importance to them?

Ignore the clouds and look for the sun in their midst. As you concentrate on the light, your mind also will become peaceful.

Don't be self-conscious about your weaknesses. Attachment and anger may still be there, but many good qualities are also present. The point is not to honor yourself for your faults but for your good qualities.

Swami Muktānanda

I welcome and honor you all as different forms of my own true Self.

When I perceived my true inner Self, I found that I was extremely lovable, that I was worthy of the greatest honor; and now as I see you, I find that you, too, are extremely lovable and worthy of the greatest honor. Therefore, I call you my dear ones, and I welcome all of you with great love.

Swami Muktānanda

FEBRUARY

The Heart Is the Hub of All Sacred Places

FEBRUARY

1

If someone were to ask me what gives meaning to my life, I would say, "The name of my Guru." I discovered everything within me by my Guru's grace.

Bhagavān Śrī Nityānanda was a perfect Guru. His essential teaching was: "The Heart is the hub of all sacred places. Go there and roam." Just by remembering and worshiping such a Master, one becomes holy.

Swami Muktānanda

FEBRUARY

2

The experience of the Heart is our connection to the inner realms. Becoming aware of the Heart is a sure sign one has attained God's blessings.

To become immersed in the knowledge of the Heart is the aim of all spiritual practices.

To experience the purity of the Heart is the blessing of all great Siddhas.

To tremble with the love of the Heart is possible only through the merits of many lifetimes.

Gurumayi Chidvilāsānanda

Out of love
the earth brings forth nectarean food.
Out of love
seasons change.
Out of love
the wind blows tirelessly.
Out of love
the good are worshiped.
Muktānanda,
love is the revelation of God.

Swami Muktānanda

There is a specific space inside the heart that is divine. Inside this space there is a light, which is the size of the thumb, and that is Consciousness.

Consciousness pervades the body from head to toe; it pervades everywhere. No place is without Consciousness. Everything is made of Consciousness.

Consciousness exists everywhere and in all beings, but specifically, it lives in the heart.

Swami Muktānanda

*I*n the *Śiva-sūtra*, Lord Śiva says:

> *The yogi who is established in a steady posture*
> *easily becomes immersed in the Heart.*

This aphorism clearly describes the way to become immersed in
the Heart. Physical posture is one aspect of this. As a meditator
grows comfortable in his posture, then his consciousness streams
into his Heart and becomes utterly still. This is when he knows
he holds eternity within him.

Gurumayi Chidvilāsānanda

ord Śiva says:

The yogi who is established in a steady posture
easily becomes immersed in the Heart.

The second aspect of this posture is very subtle. A meditator
holds his ground both within and without. He maintains a
steady stance against whatever disturbances come up —
attacks of emotion, the chattering of the mind, impulses,
daydreams, memories. Through all this he keeps his focus,
and very naturally his awareness comes to rest in the center
of his being. Then he experiences the Heart.

The Heart is sometimes described by the scriptures as
a cavern, an inner cave, and sometimes as a great lake
of Consciousness. Tranquility is its nature. It is here
that the meditator experiences the newness of life over
and over again.

Gurumayi Chidvilāsānanda

*I*t is clear that love is the original cause or source of creation, for one grows by love, lives by love, and finally even merges into eternal love.

Knowing his beloved God to be present everywhere and seeing him in all things, a *bhakta*, a devotee, leads his life happily and contentedly. Such a devotee creates a veritable heaven wherever he happens to be. Whatever is seen by the eyes, the lover perceives as his charming Beloved; whatever is heard by the ears, the lover recognizes as the gentle voice of the Beloved. With his tongue he continuously chants the sweetest melodies of love in praise of the Beloved, and his entire body feels the softest touch of his Beloved. A drop of water in the midst of an ocean beholds nothing but water on all sides. Similarly, a *bhakta* perceives God everywhere and rejoices.

How does one gain such sight and such joy? The means to behold him in this way are the incessant singing of devotional songs and rendering of loving service, which are made possible by merging the entire heart and mind, together with the intellect, ego, and senses, with the Beloved.

Immortal joy is the final achievement.

Swami Muktānanda

FEBRUARY

8

The music of the Heart sweetens your being and strengthens it at the same time.

Spellbound by the whisper of a memory that you have heard this music before, you set out in search of the cave of the Heart where the unstruck sound resonates. Seekers of all generations have walked the path before you. Those who hear the sound once again and lead their lives in harmony with it are called saints and great beings.

Gurumayi Chidvilāsānanda

In the heart there is a place filled with joy. This joy doesn't depend on anything.

The true Guru takes a disciple to that center of joy and teaches him to become established there. Obtaining this joy, the disciple becomes fearless — then he is happy not only in happiness, but in difficulties as well.

Swami Muktānanda

In this world,
the *sadguru* is your greatest friend.
The world binds you, but he sets you free.
He has given you a new birth,
so sever all bondage.
Abandon your old dwelling;
live in the new abode of the Heart.

Swami Muktānanda

The Guru can be loved so easily when a disciple keeps his or
her heart very, very simple. In this simplicity lies the key to the
highest Truth. You love the Guru the way you love a child. It is
that simple! This simplicity is the foundation of wisdom. It is
the source of inspiration. It reveals the hidden mystery. Truly,
it is pure joy.

Love the Guru with a simple heart, and you become as pure
as light.

Gurumayi Chidvilāsānanda

A disciple creates a shrine in his or her own heart.
A disciple enthrones the Guru's power in his own being.

The relationship between the Guru and the disciple is not a
physical relationship as such. The relationship between the
Guru and the disciple is one of light, where forms become
formless, where light merges into light.

The light of the disciple merges into the Guru's light
and becomes a divine flame.

Gurumayi Chidvilāsānanda

Love is man's greatest wealth.
In the form of love
God dwells in man.
Love is the nature of the Guru.
Love is a great quality
and worthy of reverence.

Let your love for God grow every day,
and let that love be without motive.
Muktānanda, love is the herb of immortality.

Swami Muktānanda

FEBRUARY

14

God's love is ever-present.

God's love is in your heart,
God's love is in my heart,
and through this love
we are connected forever.

Gurumayi Chidvilāsānanda

*T*here is after all only one language, the language of the Heart. It's full of tears, and it's full of laughter. It's full of wisdom, it's full of playfulness. It's silent, and yet it is a song of love. It is beyond ordinary words, and yet it's tangible. At times it may seem very far away, but it is actually very close.

In what language do you dream? In what language do feelings arise? In what language does a newborn baby think? In what language does a mother bird talk to her chick? In what language does water communicate with the lilies that grow in it?
The language of the Heart.

This is the Truth.

Gurumayi Chidvilāsānanda

*W*hen you look upon all people equally,
and when you have love for everything
around you, that is another way of
expressing your devotion to the Guru.

Swami Muktānanda

FEBRUARY

17

As soon as you welcome someone with love, God is alive in your own heart.

In the Sanskrit language the word for welcome is *svāgatam*, and *svāgatam* literally means "I have come. I have arrived." So who are you really welcoming? Yourself. There is no other. Only the One who dwells within us all.

Gurumayi Chidvilāsānanda

FEBRUARY

18

*T*he only body God has
is the body of love.

Swami Muktānanda

In pure laughter you get in touch with your own love,
your own joy. And it is this pure laughter, laughter
with complete freedom, that beautifies God's creation.
This is what really brings greatness into one's life.
When people laugh from the heart, you experience
God in their laughter.

Gurumayi Chidvilāsānanda

FEBRUARY

20

There is a center within the human being that is a reservoir of love. When it overflows, you cry — that's just how it is. When the heart is filled with love, there is no language. No language can communicate love. Tears are the only medium through which we can express our love. Because there is no technique and no language, peacefully we have to cry. There is no other way.

Swami Muktānanda

*E*ntering the heart is like coming into the center of the sun. There is no more *you;* there is nothing except the iridescent force of that light.

When you are in the center of the sun, there is no way to block its light. It streams through you and around you. So by entering your own heart, you make the whole world a better paradise.

Gurumayi Chidvilāsānanda

*T*hroughout the centuries every saint has spoken about the inner intoxication, the inner love. If you try to hear about this with your physical ears alone, you may not be able to listen.

But when your being is dyed in the color of love, when you learn to live in the abode of the saints, you don't want to hear anything else, you don't want to see anything else. You just want love and nothing but love.

Gurumayi Chidvilāsānanda

*W*hen a person truly loves the Guru, even though the eyes are looking outside, the gaze has turned within.

The Guru doesn't even have to look at you to know; it is felt in the heart. Your eyes touch the Guru's heart, and wherever the Guru goes, your love is felt inside.

Gurumayi Chidvilāsānanda

*A*bhinavagupta, the great sage of Kashmir Shaivism, says: "Hṛdaya, the Heart, literally means 'mainstay' or 'resting place.'"

According to the sages, all of life, the great chain of being that inhabits the universe, comes to rest in the light of Consciousness, in Paramaśiva, the supreme Heart of all.

When you learn to take refuge in the Heart, the perfect serenity of Paramaśiva will renew you completely.

Gurumayi Chidvilāsānanda

Hṛdaya, the Heart. Take refuge in the Heart.

Sometimes when you least expect it, you are given a
greater vision of the true nature of the Heart. It may
take the form of an explosion of light — more brilliant
than anything you've ever seen before — as if the heavens
blazed with a thousand suns, all of them inside yourself.
It may take the form of limitless darkness, softer than
any night. Some people may experience the Heart as an
ancient, ever-existing presence. Then you can see the Truth
shining in their eyes, and their voices ring with exultation
when they say, "The Heart — I know what it is! Somehow
I know that it's me!"

No matter what form the vision takes or how long it lasts,
it makes a seeker cry out with great joy: "How astonishing!
How amazing! Extraordinary! Unimaginable! Blessed am I!"

These experiences bring about real and lasting transformation.

Gurumayi Chidvilāsānanda

*T*hrough intense, deep meditation you reach a state that is beyond thought, beyond change, beyond imagination, beyond differences and duality. Once you can stay in that state for a while and come out of it without losing any of it, then the inner divine love will begin to pour through you.

You will not see people as different, separate individuals. You will see your own Self in everyone around you. Then the flow of love from within you will be constant and unbroken.

Swami Muktānanda

FEBRUARY

27

Nothing in this world can be compared to the ecstasy of a great soul.

Simply remembering one who is the embodiment of love fills your entire being with the great one's light.

Gurumayi Chidvilāsānanda

Grace flowed from Swami Muktānanda as easily as rainwater cascades down a mountainside.

As grace streamed out of his being to touch the heart of a seeker, anything that was standing in the way dissolved in his love.

Gurumayi Chidvilāsānanda

*G*od must have a reason why he has put each one of us on this planet at this time. So live up to God's wishes, live up to God's ideas. Experience the strength and courage, the love and generosity that God has placed inside your heart.

Remember the Heart again and again. "The Heart is the hub of all sacred places. Go there and roam."

Gurumayi Chidvilāsānanda

MARCH

Make the Mind Your Friend

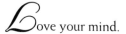ove your mind.

The mind is the friend
who leads you by its restlessness
to search for God.

The mind is the instrument
by which you detect
the inner world.

Swami Muktānanda

The mind is actually an extension of the supreme Self.
It is a form of the Self that turns toward the outer world,
so that living beings can understand all things
and speak of them as expressions of the Absolute
and function in this world.

When it turns inward, the mind is a vehicle
to travel back to the supreme Self.

Gurumayi Chidvilāsānanda

One of the *sūtras* of the *Pratyabhijñā-hṛdayam* says:

The supreme energy, descending from the stage of universal
Consciousness, becomes the mind through the process of contraction.

In the beginning the mind is pure Consciousness. It is
constantly in an expanded state, completely reveling in delight.
As this pure awareness becomes contracted, it also acquires
limitations, and then it is known as the mind. Even then,
it doesn't really forget its original nature; it remembers it is
pure Consciousness.

This is why you have longing. This is why you say to yourself,
"There is something more to life. There is something much
more beautiful."

Who tells you that?

It is the mind remembering its original state. And this
memory is very strong. Over and over again it reminds you:
attain the state of pure Consciousness; attain that pure,
great state.

Gurumayi Chidvilāsānanda

*C*onsciousness, the divine energy, has created the universe out of its own being, without taking the help of anything outside itself. In the same way, when Consciousness becomes the mind by assuming limitations, it begins to create endless mental universes.

There are many outer universes, but they are all contained in Consciousness. In the same way, the universes that vibrate in the mind should not be seen as different from Consciousness.

No matter what thoughts and images arise in the mind, be aware that there is no concrete material from which they are being manifested. They are simply a phantasmagoria of Consciousness, and no matter how many worlds of desires, wishes, and positive and negative thoughts your mind creates, you should realize that they are all a play of Consciousness.

Swami Muktānanda

MARCH

5

*O*nce you understand that the mind was born of Consciousness and is not different from Consciousness, then you can make friends with your mind.

Gurumayi Chidvilāsānanda

The One you are looking for is beyond all thought.
He is experienced when thought ceases.

That is God, where the mind cannot reach,
where speech cannot reach,
where the intellect cannot reach.

Where the mind merges all its thoughts,
there God begins to shine.

When the mind becomes completely still,
then God reveals himself with all his love.

Swami Muktānanda

The mind has to become quiet
to hear the words of God.

Gurumayi Chidvilāsānanda

The experience of God lies within your mind.

When you attain God, who lies within your mind, separation disappears and union takes place. You become God, you become the Truth. When this experience occurs, the sages call out, "I am God! I am God!" Their experience arises from the divine state, beyond the boundaries of the physical or mental worlds.

It is from this awareness that Bābā Muktānanda says, "Meditate on your own Self. Honor and worship your own Self. Kneel to your own Self. God dwells within you as you."

Gurumayi Chidvilāsānanda

*B*y meditating more and more, you learn the knack of stilling all your thoughts. Even if a thought-wave were to arise, however, it is only the thought-free Being who is becoming that thought.

An intelligent person knows that water becomes ice. He doesn't have to melt ice over a fire to see the water. He sees the water even when it is ice. In the same way, an enlightened being knows it is the Consciousness beyond thought that becomes all thoughts. He sees thoughts as waves and eddies in that ocean of Consciousness and he remains drunk on inner bliss.

Swami Muktānanda

*I*n the realized state the mind doesn't function as mere mind; it functions with all the power of pure Consciousness. It becomes stable and free of thoughts; it becomes still. Unhappiness is nothing but the net of thoughts, and when we go beyond thoughts, we experience supreme bliss.

Moreover, as the mind becomes one with the Self, it acquires the power of the Self.

Swami Muktānanda

After *śaktipāt* occurs, the Śakti purifies the mind and the heart.

When the mind becomes free from all thoughts and doubts, when it becomes still, then know that the mind has become pure. The fewer thoughts you have, the purer you become. Ultimately, the mind merges into the Self; it is not destroyed, but it becomes absorbed in the Self.

The mind will be with you as long as the body exists. But when it becomes pure, then the mind will act as a friend to you — it won't be your enemy. It will play and sport within you with great joy.

Swami Muktānanda

*O*nce you realize that the mind is not a small, insignificant thing, once you experience it as pure Consciousness, you never want to lose the experience.

This is why the great beings always pray that their minds may remain pristine and clear, as transparent as the dawn.

Gurumayi Chidvilāsānanda

*W*ho is it who knows your feelings? It is the Witness of the mind, the Witness of your emotions.

There is no conscious knowing in emotions. Emotions cannot know themselves. The Knower of the emotions is different from the emotions. Whatever feelings you have, whether good or bad, the Knower of these feelings is different from them.

To know the Witness is realization.

Swami Muktānanda

Life is a great play. It contains countless names and forms and unexpected events. To make life very full, every flavor is required.

Now this is where your greatness is put to the test. You must remain a Witness of it all.

If you want to experience serenity and perceive the Truth, be a Witness. Remain a Witness at all times.

Gurumayi Chidvilāsānanda

*A*s you sit for meditation, you watch the activities of the mind as if you were watching a movie, and you learn to become careful about certain thoughts.

You watch each thought as it comes. Sometimes a thought is complete and sometimes it is not complete. And as you watch, you can really see which thoughts create suffering and which create great joy. As you understand this, you are able to accept the fact that you create and destroy your own world. In this way you become vigilant very naturally.

Bit by bit, you learn to apply the patience and the vigilance you obtain through meditation in order to quiet the mind whenever you want to.

Gurumayi Chidvilāsānanda

$\mathcal{J}$f you want to have the vision of your own supreme Self, then become like a clear, calm lake that reflects the moon in its fullness.

Gurumayi Chidvilāsānanda

The Heart is the resting place of the mind. When you release the mind from unnecessary thoughts, very naturally it flows into the Heart. This is when meditation takes place of its own accord, spontaneously.

A mind that has united with the Heart is called great because it generates golden ideas. Such a mind can turn an ordinary moment into a divine occasion.

Gurumayi Chidvilāsānanda

*A*gain and again this has been made clear:
as long as the mind does not rest in the Heart,
it gives birth to illusory worlds, illusory concepts.

An untrained mind is constantly agitated.
Everything it thinks is colored by limited ideas.
It is like a butterfly fluttering in a closed bottle:
wherever the wings touch, they leave their color
on the glass, creating their own impressions.
This is the state of an agitated mind.

However, when the mind rests in the Heart,
all barriers break down, and it experiences
the immense Consciousness. All latent impressions
then fade into nothingness. Therefore, it is
the duty of a seeker to bring the mind
continually back to its source.

Gurumayi Chidvilāsānanda

MARCH

19

When the mind merges into the Heart,
the mind is your friend.

Gurumayi Chidvilāsānanda

One of the greatest practices for bringing the mind under control is mantra repetition. A mantra is a cosmic word or sound vibration. In fact, mantra is the vibration of the Self. It is the true speech of the Self arising from within.

The mantra is one with God and very easily puts us in touch with the God within. There is no difference between God and his Name.

Mantra has the full power of God. Above all, it has the power to purify the mind and bring it to the Self.

Swami Muktānanda

*T*he vibration of the mind and the vibration of the mantra are one and the same. That which pulsates within the mind and within the mantra is a living force. It is Consciousness itself.

A seeker whose mind is constantly absorbed in the mantra finds that the mind and the mantra are no longer two different entities. As the scriptures say: *cittaṁ mantraḥ,* "The mind is mantra." When such a state arises, a seeker is blissful. He does not have to make an effort to recite the mantra; he can *hear* the mantra within himself and everywhere.

When the mind is the mantra, all your prayers bear fruit.

Gurumayi Chidvilāsānanda

22

When a ship sails across a body of water, it leaves a wake of choppy, turbulent waves on the surface, but it is not concerned about that. The ship doesn't turn around and come back to try to smooth the ripples out of the sea. It lets the wind fill its sails and turns its prow toward its destination.

So the thoughts that come up in your mind are no more than ripples on the surface of your consciousness. Let the mantra carry you forward like a magnificent ship. Let the vibrations of the mantra fill your sails and bring you home.

Gurumayi Chidvilāsānanda

A great mind creates great things. A great mind is like a fountain of fresh water.

Just as the physical body is kept in good shape through disciplined movement, the mind is made finer by beautiful reflections.

When the mind becomes finer and finer, as subtle as the breath, it can enter the kingdom of Truth.

Gurumayi Chidvilāsānanda

*A*s long as many thoughts play in the mind, it is very difficult to bring the mind under control and make it still.

So the best thing to do is to have one strong thought: "I am the Self." This is called *pūrṇo'ham-vimarśa,* pure I-consciousness.

Gurumayi Chidvilāsānanda

Teach the mind good things about your own Self. Talk to the mind about the love of your own Self. Speak to the mind and tell it, "I am God, I am perfect, I am the highest love. Citi Śakti, cosmic Consciousness, is blazing within me."

Keep telling your mind, "My inner Self is a flame of the divine Self, it is a flame of God."

Thought has immense power. One person who thinks like this can make hundreds of others think good thoughts.

Swami Muktānanda

*D*on't worry about anything.
Forget what has happened in the past.
Don't let past memories come into your mind.
Let a new life begin.

Swami Muktānanda

*N*othing ever happens without your secretly wishing for it. Some time or another, you must have thought about that and invited it into existence.

Since it is the nature of the mind to think incessantly, give the mind something very pure and auspicious to contemplate. This is why we love to chant the names of God.

Gurumayi Chidvilāsānanda

The more still and one-pointed the mind becomes, the more work it is able to do.

If someone dams a stream and stops its flow, that stream becomes a lake with enough water to satisfy the thirst of thousands of people.

When the flow of the mind is controlled, it can accomplish anything.

Swami Muktānanda

A mind that has been purified by the love within, that has been burned in the immaculate fire of yoga, can infuse life into a sick person. The concentrated energy of such a mind can give meaning to the life of a person who feels lost. It can heal wounds.

When you have not matured, you experience much restlessness. However, when the mind has matured in the knowledge of God, in the knowledge of one's own Self, it can create shelter and give support to those who long for the Truth.

Gurumayi Chidvilāsānanda

*J*ust as the world of an individual is the product of his mind, the universe is the product of the mind of the Lord.

In the *Bhagavad-gītā*, the Lord says that all the creatures of the world arose from his mind.

According to the great philosophy of Kashmir Shaivism, the universe is the sport of the mind of the supreme Lord. Shaivism says that in the beginning the Lord was alone. Then he had the thought, "Let me become many," and from his thought the world manifested.

The universe is contained in the cosmic mind, and the mind of the individual is a portion of it. Therefore, the Upaniṣads say, "Worship the mind as a great deity."

Swami Muktānanda

A good mind can rebuild an entire universe.

Filled with the love of God,
a good mind can withstand a raging storm.
A good mind can offer love
without any strings attached.
A good mind can inspire others.
A good mind is like fertile soil:
whatever you plant there
grows into something beneficial to mankind.

A good mind is filled with the love of God.

Gurumayi Chidvilāsānanda

APRIL

⤚

Kuṇḍalinī Śakti,
The Power of the Universe

APRIL

1

*T*he mighty Kuṇḍalinī Śakti is the vital force of the universe.

As fire, she gives heat; as the sun, she gives light; as rain, she brings showers; as wind, she blows everywhere. She is the earth. She exists in the form of all material objects.

No words can describe her. She is a woman; she is a man. She is everything in the world. She is that which exists and that which does not exist.

Swami Muktānanda

*K*undalinī Śakti is a great power. She is the secret of the universe. When a horse gallops or a fish darts, when a bird swoops out of the sky or lightning flashes, when a seed suddenly sprouts into a tender green leaf, and a mighty waterfall cascades, there is so much sheer power and speed in these things. Yet it is just an iota, a tiny reflection, of the playfulness of Kundalinī, the great energy. There is such tremendous beauty in high, snow-covered mountains like the Himalayas, the Swiss Alps, Mount Fuji. The sight of them takes your breath away; it ushers you into a pure world of stillness. And yet, even this is a mere whisper of the might and the majesty of the Kundalinī energy, the great power within a human being.

The charm of a baby's smile; the way buds open, quivering into tender flowers; the texture of silk or velvet; a breath of fresh air — all this is still a minute reflection of the Kundalinī Śakti, the great power within. There are millions of incredibly beautiful things in the world of nature. Yet all of this is like a grain of sand compared to the intensity, and also the gentleness, of the Kundalinī energy, the great power within.

Gurumayi Chidvilāsānanda

The ancient sages glorified the goddess Kuṇḍalinī as the divine Mother. She is the source, the womb of the world, the origin of everything that is, and everything that is not. Kuṇḍalinī is both compassionate and terrifying at the same time. She is the greatest giver and the most ferocious slayer, simultaneously. What does she give? The freedom of the Self. What does she slay? Everything that holds us down.

Kuṇḍalinī Śakti is the force that gave birth to the sun and the moon and all the galaxies of the universe — to the great Light that makes them shine.

Salutations to Kuṇḍalinī, the universal Mother!

Gurumayi Chidvilāsānanda

She is the power of becoming,
released out of the eternal Being
and expressing Herself through all names,
all forms, and all changes
that we call the world.
Indeed, She is the most magnificent power —
Śrī Kuṇḍalinī Śakti — of the supreme Reality.

To set this Kuṇḍalinī into operation
within an individual being
is known as *śaktipāt*.
And one who gives *śaktipāt dīkṣā*, initiation,
is a Guru.

Swami Muktānanda

*W*ith the initiation called *śaktipāt*, the Guru transmits his
own fully awakened, conscious energy into the disciple.
Through this action, the Guru ignites the same Kuṇḍalinī
energy that lies dormant in the disciple, waiting to catch fire.
Putting this divine act into words makes it sound so simple
and easy, but what actually happens within, hidden from the
senses, is something marvelous. It can only be deciphered by
the deepest part of you, yet your whole being is rejuvenated by
its light. This unimaginable *prasād*, this divine gift — *śaktipāt*
dīkṣā from the Guru — creates a bond between the two of
you that can never be broken.

Gurumayi Chidvilāsānanda

APRIL

6

---

*F*or countless ages, *śaktipāt* has been used as a secret means of initiation by the great sages. To transmit one's own glory and luster of divine enlightenment into a disciple and give him an instantaneous direct experience of Brahman, the eternal Spirit, is the secret meaning of *śaktipāt*.

Swami Muktānanda

APRIL

7

Śaktipāt dīkṣā is the master key that allows entry into the temple of Truth.

Gurumayi Chidvilāsānanda

Śaktipāt initiation, the awakening of Kuṇḍalinī Śakti,
is the supreme act of the Master's grace. It is the lightning
bolt that reveals the greatest treasure within. It is the ultimate
gesture of compassion, the breath of the Absolute that breaks
the chains of endless death and rebirth and sets you free once
and for all.

When Kuṇḍalinī Śakti is awakened by the Master's grace,
the knot of the heart is released. All karmas, all sins, are washed
away and the pure Being is revealed within. This Being is the
embodiment of wisdom, light, and truth.

Gurumayi Chidvilāsānanda

Śaktipāt is like a volcano erupting. The brilliant red-orange
molten lava that pours out of the crater is like the love that
is suddenly released from the core of your being. This great
love streams into the ocean of your life, seeps all the way
to the bottom, where it continues to burn. Water cannot
put this fire out. The current of events that beats against it
like waves cannot stop it from burning nor quench the heat
of this love.

Gurumayi Chidvilāsānanda

APRIL

10

It is said that all the three worlds are lit by the light of the sun. In the same way, one who receives the great blessing of Śakti perceives this entire universe as pervaded by her. He sees all the worlds illumined in the rays of the Śakti, who leaps up with bliss.

Swami Muktānanda

When Kuṇḍalinī is awakened, sometimes you are completely aware of her manifestations in dramatic or in subtle forms. And other times you are not aware at all; nevertheless, something is happening. Sooner or later, you begin to notice changes in the way you think, in the way you feel, in the way you do things. All of a sudden, you realize you are a different person. There is a greater beauty that is unfolding within you, a greater understanding. Somebody speaks, and it opens a new dimension. You understand something that you never understood before.

How wonderful is the play of Kuṇḍalinī Śakti! When she manifests in each one's being, she gives such clarity to the intellect, she gives such strength to the heart. She makes a person become kinder, more compassionate, more understanding.

Salutations to Kuṇḍalinī Śakti, the Mother of the inner universe.

Gurumayi Chidvilāsānanda

APRIL

12

*K*undalinī is a great source of motivation and inspiration. She makes a writer a better writer, a doctor a better doctor, a statesman a better statesman, a businessman a better businessman, a mother a better mother. All talents and skills lie in her womb, and when Kundalinī is awakened, these abilities manifest in our lives. Kundalinī improves whatever needs improvement; where we have imperfections, she strengthens and balances us.

It is said that worldly pleasure and spiritual perfection can never be found together. But this is not the case when we follow the path of Kundalinī. A scripture says, "When one walks on the path of the supremely beautiful Kundalinī, liberation and worldly enjoyments go hand in hand." This world, after all, is Kundalinī's creation; it is Kundalinī herself. So it should not be surprising that Kundalinī is able to take care of every aspect of our lives.

Swami Muktānanda

*J*ust as you create a very strong box to hold something
precious, delicate, and rare, in the same way you naturally
want to create the perfect conditions within yourself for
this sublime energy. You want to help it unfold and expand.
So as your destiny is affected by the inner fire, the awakened
energy, you are drawn to contemplation. You make an effort
to see through the effects to the causes. You contemplate.
Why did you do what you did? What impelled you to go in a
certain direction? How can you shed the costly illusions that
set you on the wrong path? Why is your mind still attracted
to the same old patterns? Why can't your heart hold the
knowledge of God?

When you contemplate these things, it fans the fire within.
It makes you want to do something about them, to change
your way of being and thinking. Through this contemplation
you stop blaming the world, blaming God. All you want now
is to drink God's grace, to keep your heart open to receive
his grace.

Gurumayi Chidvilāsānanda

APRIL

14

*O*Mother Kuṇḍalinī, you are the almighty sustainer
of the human body. You are the embodiment of Citi.
You are the pure-souled Guru of all great Gurus.
Enthroned on the Guru's seat, in the two-petaled
lotus between the eyebrows, you secure for your
disciples what they don't already have and preserve
what they already possess.

O Yoginī Kuṇḍalinī, you are the supreme deity of
spiritual aspirants.

Swami Muktānanda

$\mathcal{I}$t is Her nature to dance with great joy, and therefore there is always a gentle motion, a slight sway in your being, even when you are absolutely still.

As She gently moves in and around you, She sings to Herself. So listen to the sound She makes. Whatever you hear, every sound manifests from Her. As you become absorbed in the inner sound of the Śakti, you glide into meditation. Your breath is Her whisper. Your breath is Her song. Your breath is Her dance. To please the Śakti, to awaken Her within us, and to keep Her glory manifest in our being, we chant Her own song to Her — the sound *oṁ*.

Gurumayi Chidvilāsānanda

*K*undalinī Śakti is so deft in her own creation. Not only does she create but she creates everything upon her own being. A potter makes pots using clay, but she creates everything out of her own being, within her own being, and upon her own being. Therefore, she is called both transcendent and immanent. She is in the universe, she is also beyond the universe. She is within everything, yet she transcends everything also. She is both the womb and the child. What an incredible, infinite play this is!

Gurumayi Chidvilāsānanda

*T*ruly speaking, Śakti is the most precious of all. She is day, and she is night. She is the sun, and she is the moon. She is high tide, and she is low tide. She is loss, and she is gain. She is the power in all that exists and all that does not exist. She is a moment, and she is infinite aeons. She makes the eyes blink and the lips move. She bestows fortune and misfortune. If you know her, you can smile at her play. If you don't know her, you live in misery. She must be known. Let's put it this way: she *wants* to be known. She is the Holy Spirit. She is sacred. She touches all, but remains untouched. She sees all, but remains unseen. She belongs to everyone, but no one owns her. Without her there is no universe.

Gurumayi Chidvilāsānanda

There is a knot in the heart that makes you experience yourself as small, though you are great. This knot makes you experience suffering, even though you are nothing but bliss. It is because of this knot that you consider yourself to be made of matter, though you are made of Consciousness. The knot in the heart gives rise to this kind of wrong understanding over and over, and after giving rise to it, nourishes it and keeps it firm.

In meditation this knot must be cut out through the surgery of Kuṇḍalinī. It is not a physical knot; it is a psychological knot. It is called *māyā*, or illusion. This knot in the heart can be burned up by the fire of Kuṇḍalinī. When this knot is gone, all of a sudden the inner being is filled with light and you begin to laugh. It is this knot that causes everyone to suffer. The purpose of the Guru's grace is to burn it up.

Swami Muktānanda

APRIL

19

If you put a crystal in a fire, it cracks inside. As long as you keep it in the fire, it continues to crack into tinier and tinier parts. The crystal is still whole, but on the inside it becomes fragmented and reflects the light like a diamond with many facets. In the same way, as the inner awakening takes place, the fire of Consciousness burns away all impurities, all negativities. You are still in the body, but inside, everything becomes Consciousness, everything becomes light.

In the crystal, you can see all the colors sparkling, and it is the same with this body. As it goes on burning in the fire of love, the fire of Truth, it becomes Consciousness, nothing but Consciousness.

Gurumayi Chidvilāsānanda

A seeker's attitude toward life cannot be passive. You are not just sitting there laid back, watching the drama of life unfold. Just the opposite. Nourished by the ongoing experience of the Śakti, you participate wholeheartedly in God's creation, but at the same time you remain detached and never forget that all this is God's play.

Gurumayi Chidvilāsānanda

APRIL

21

If you learn how to pay attention to the awakened Kuṇḍalinī, she continually guides you. She is a living torch that guides you on your path.

Gurumayi Chidvilāsānanda

*A*s you pursue this self-born yoga, as the inner Śakti unfolds, you reach the *sahasrāra*, the topmost spiritual center at the crown of the head. This is the culmination of your spiritual journey, and here the light of the Self reveals itself. In the *sahasrāra* there is a divine effulgence. That light has the radiance of a thousand suns. In that center, there is no pain and no pleasure. Only the bliss of Consciousness exists there. In the center of that divine effulgence in the *sahasrāra*, there is a tiny subtle blue light, which yogis call the *nīla-bindu*, the Blue Pearl. Watching this tender, infinitely fascinating light, you become aware of your true glory. Though smaller than a sesame seed, the Blue Pearl contains the entire universe. It is the light of God, the form of God within you. This is the divinity, this is the greatness that lies within a human being. This is the true wonder of humanity. Therefore, perceive that light.

Swami Muktānanda

*A*s you inhale and exhale, pray to Kuṇḍalinī Śakti: "Make me worthy to perceive my own light. Make me worthy to perceive the Blue Pearl, which is my very Self."

Let there be humility and devotion in your prayer to Kuṇḍalinī Śakti: "Make me worthy to perceive the divine light. Make me worthy to perceive the Blue Pearl, which is my inner Self."

Gurumayi Chidvilāsānanda

*W*hen the Blue Pearl comes and stands in front of the meditator, it can grow and grow and grow until it becomes so big that the whole universe is just a dot in its vast expanse.

Divine music emerges from its inner vibrations. It intoxicates you as you listen to it. And as you gaze at it, you see streams of tiny, tiny particles flowing from it to every part of the body. They bring such delightful sensations that you feel like dancing. This is the purpose of taking birth in a human form.

Swami Muktānanda

APRIL

25

*W*hen Kuṇḍalinī is awakened and the inner fire is kindled, you can actually see within this fire the sound of "I am" pulsating.

It is not a mere thought, it is not a mere fantasy, it is not a mere idea of "I am." When you watch the inner fire, you actually *see* this sound.

Gurumayi Chidvilāsānanda

*T*he scriptures say:
Kuṇḍalinī is of the form of mantra.

The mantra is the most visible and tangible form of that great
power. Kuṇḍalinī is so beautiful and, at the same time, so
independent that no tactic of the ego can capture her. That
is utterly impossible. She has to be praised with a pure heart.
She must be allowed to reveal her true form in her own good
time. You must be patient.

As you wait for her to manifest, the best way to invoke her
is by using one of her very own forms, and that is the mantra.
The mantra is the best solution.

Gurumayi Chidvilāsānanda

*A*lthough She assumes many forms, She is one.

When this unity awareness arises from within, you begin to sway in the supreme bliss of the ultimate state. Through the grace of Śakti, as She is awakened within, you realize that She also permeates everything outside.

Through the grace of Śakti, you can come to experience Śakti.

Gurumayi Chidvilāsānanda

APRIL

28

*J*ust as a river, after flowing for a long time, merges in
the ocean and becomes the ocean, when Kuṇḍalinī has
finished her work and is stabilized in the *sahasrāra*, the
spiritual center at the crown of the head, you become
completely immersed in God. All your impurities are
destroyed, and you take complete rest in the Self. The
veil that made you see duality drops away, and you
experience the world as a blissful play of Kuṇḍalinī, a
sport of God's energy. You see the universe as supremely
blissful light, undifferentiated from yourself, and you
remain unshakable in this awareness. This is the state
of liberation, the state of perfection.

Swami Muktānanda

*E*verything in your life is the Śakti.
Knowing this, you become liberated.

Gurumayi Chidvilāsānanda

*D*ear Siddha students!

You are all rays of Siddha beings. You are all taking part in the play of Citi Śakti. She is active within you. May you become saturated with Consciousness in the world you live in, which is also the embodiment of Consciousness, and, merging in Citi, become Citi. May your minds attain complete repose in the Goddess Citi's realm, which is nothing but stillness.

This is my blessing.

Swami Muktānanda

MAY

Only One Who Obeys Can Command

MAY

1

*J*n the Vedas it is said: "Only one who obeys can command." Only one who has attained something within himself can help others.

If a person hasn't practiced something for himself, then no matter how much he tries to teach others, no matter how much he tries to convince others of his point of view, they just cannot understand what he's saying. They won't believe him.

For this reason, first you should fill yourself with good qualities. You should attain That. Then you will be able to make the people around you and your society understand what you are speaking about.

First of all, your *sādhanā* should bear fruit for you; only then can it bear fruit for many other people.

Swami Muktānanda

*Y*ou can neither obey nor command unless you surrender. You cannot hold on to your smallness and say, "I am serving."

This is something one should understand from the very beginning. One should learn to surrender to the higher power that exists within oneself.

If a seeker is true to himself and really wants to know God, then he must abandon his lower self to the higher Truth.

Gurumayi Chidvilāsānanda

God dwells within you.
If you surrender to him in your heart,
you will become him.

Swami Muktānanda

Mumukṣutva is the determination to attain liberation. It is this burning desire that makes a person seek the Truth. Such a person is called a *mumukṣu*, one who is willing to sacrifice himself in order to know the greater power within, to acquire divine knowledge.

A true *mumukṣu* wants to break through all the barriers that keep him chained to his own limitations. With a longing for freedom that can never be forgotten, he is determined to become one with the Truth. So even a tinge of ego is painful to him. Tirelessly, a *mumukṣu* seeks to abandon himself to the will of God.

Be a *mumukṣu*: yearn with your whole heart to become one with the great Truth.

Gurumayi Chidvilāsānanda

*I*f your senses have not been purified, you fall prey to the delusion, "Should I obey or should I command?" This dilemma need not arise when the scriptures give such a direct message: "Only one who obeys can command."

Commanding is not giving orders. Obeying is not groveling in the dust. Obeying is imbibing the Truth and commanding is being the Truth.

Gurumayi Chidvilāsānanda

MAY

6

I was always ready to obey the command of my Guru.
I followed the path he showed me, never wondering when
I would reach perfection, never asking where the road was
leading. Whatever path he put me on, I followed, regarding
it as his command.

Since I followed in that way, I reached where I should have
reached. I didn't look to one side or the other, nor did I bother
about small things. I just kept going straight ahead. I found
what I had to find. I became what I was to become, and in the
becoming, there was nothing lacking.

Swami Muktānanda

In Kashmir Shaivism there is an esoteric text called the
Śiva-sūtra. One of its aphorisms says:

> gururupāyaḥ
> *The Guru is the means.*

The literal meaning of the word *guru* is deceptively simple.
The first syllable *gu* means "darkness," and *ru* means "light."
So the Guru is a being who dispels darkness and bestows light.
The Guru removes ignorance and instills knowledge of the Self
in a seeker.

A Guru is someone who has allowed himself to be a disciple
and has gone through the whole process of eradicating himself.
A Guru is someone who has consented to be annihilated by the
grace of his own Guru, who has seen the Truth, and who lives
only to fulfill the command his Guru gave him.

Gurumayi Chidvilāsānanda

A true devotee
is one who has merged his identity with God;

a perfect yogi
is one who is always in communion
with the inner Self;

and, likewise, a true disciple
is one whose soul is forever united with the Guru.

Swami Muktānanda

To the Guru,
whose very nature is bliss,
through whose bounty
the seeker's mind
forgets worldly sufferings
and the seeker's intellect
attains steadfast wisdom;

through whose grace
the heart is entirely filled with love
and begins to perceive ambrosial joy
pervading everywhere;

through whose supreme gift of *śaktipāt*
the intricacies of yoga
become automatically intelligible
and one reaches the final state of *samādhi*,
the transcendental bliss of Consciousness
that lies beyond the void;

to such a munificent Guru
the disciple will ever remain indebted.

Swami Muktānanda

MAY

10

_As_ you follow the path shown by the Guru, a natural surrender must take place.

If you try to bend a dry stick, it breaks; but try to bend a vine, and it yields to your wishes. So surrender is the flexibility that is required in the Guru-disciple relationship.

The Guru's surrender is the bestowal of grace. In the form of obedience, the disciple imbibes the grace.

Gurumayi Chidvilāsānanda

The scriptures say all attainments come from obeying the Guru. It is a sweet surrender. The Guru has attained the Truth, so obeying the Guru is obeying the Truth. And this very power of obedience invokes the power to command. The disciplined senses that have obeyed the Truth, the Guru's command, can direct the course of others' lives.

When you understand the greatness of obedience, there is no desire to command, really. It is just a quality you have; your very presence is commanding.

Gurumayi Chidvilāsānanda

MAY

12

The Guru is a benevolent force. The Guru's entire being vibrates with love. The Guru's sole purpose is to elevate the disciple to a higher state of consciousness. Little by little, the Guru transforms the disciple until he becomes the embodiment of perfection.

Gurumayi Chidvilāsānanda

To surrender to the Guru means to try constantly to imbibe the Guru's instructions. Jñāneśvar Mahārāj said that a true disciple is one who washes his mind in the Guru's words. He holds the Guru's knowledge in his heart, identifies himself with the Guru, and remains immersed in the Guru with the awareness that the Guru is his own inner Self. He surrenders to the Guru his sense of limitation. He merges his smallness into the Guru's vastness.

Only this is true discipleship, and a person who becomes a disciple like this does not remain stuck in discipleship. He does not become small and weak. Instead, he becomes established in the state the Guru has attained.

Swami Muktānanda

When a disciple completely surrenders to the Guru,
his reward is total identity with the Guru.

Swami Muktānanda

It is not necessary that you live with the Guru to surrender to the Guru. What is necessary is that you have love for the Guru and that you have an interest in the Truth.

Swami Muktānanda

MAY

16

Swami Muktānanda did not just consider a few mountains to be sacred, or a few lakes, or a few places, or a few objects, or a few words, or a few trees, or a few people. For him, everything was his Guru, everything was God. God was the blood that flowed through his veins. God was the food that nourished him. If he walked outside, it was to see God in nature. If he sat quietly, it was to listen to God's wisdom. If he spoke, it was to express God's message. To see God, to hear God, to experience God, to love God — that was his whole reason for living. His intense love for his Guru allowed him to melt entirely into God until there was no separation between them. This is why many of Bābā's devotees always felt that Bābā and Bhagavān Nityānanda were the same. Swami Muktānanda had merged completely into Bhagavān Nityānanda, his Guru. And wherever he looked, he saw his Guru, he saw God.

Bābā made one promise to his Guru; that was, "I am your disciple." And today we are reaping the fruits of that one promise.

Gurumayi Chidvilāsānanda

MAY

17

The greatest saints are always the greatest disciples.

Gurumayi Chidvilāsānanda

MAY

18

$\mathcal{D}$iscipleship is a *sādhanā* that never really ends. It may reach its perfection; nevertheless, it never ends. It continually unfolds itself in this supreme perfection. Even though the disciple merges into the Guru and becomes the Guru, discipleship remains intact.

Gurumayi Chidvilāsānanda

*E*ven now when my Bābā is no longer in his physical form,
I follow his commands most faithfully.

Swami Muktānanda

In the final state, both obedience and command are in perfect harmony. The power to obey is as strong as the power to command. You cannot do one without the other. These powers to obey and command arise from pure love. Where there is love, there is humility.

Through the power of humility, a great one obeys and commands.

Gurumayi Chidvilāsānanda

O Self of all,
  I take refuge in you.
  I ask nothing of you.
  Grant me whatever boon you choose.
  I will be totally content
  with whatever you give me,
  whether it be pain or pleasure.
  Do whatever you will,
  but keep me in your presence.

Swami Muktānanda

Nobody's going to tell you when you have become a disciple. It is something that happens on the inside. It's the seeker who yearns for this. As long as there's no yearning, no longing, it doesn't happen. It is something that is put into action by the seeker; the Guru knows and you know, without telling each other. It is the inner connection.

A lot of seekers serve, a lot of seekers meditate, a lot of seekers chant. Through one of these means, each one is able to recognize the existing connection between the two hearts. So it's a matter of recognition on your part, rather than someone coming to tell you, "Today you are a disciple!"

Gurumayi Chidvilāsānanda

*M*any people ask me to explain surrender.

When you do not understand the secret of surrender, you do not feel like surrendering.

When understanding arises, surrender takes place of its own accord. You do not have to do anything.

Swami Muktānanda

The Guru's direction should be obeyed because there is great mystery behind the Guru's command. Realization is not something that descends from the blue sky and enters us. For a disciple, realization is achieved through obedience to the Guru's command.

You should strive again and again to be faithful to the Guru's word.

Swami Muktānanda

The *Bhagavad-gītā* says that to surrender all the fruits of one's actions is a great practice.

Surrendering all your actions to God means that when you listen to something, you listen for God. When you eat food, you eat for God. As you live in this world, you do that for God too. Whatever you do is for God.

Swami Muktānanda

All the sages and saints urge seekers to lose themselves in
That—the source of all happiness—so that all their actions
in this world may spring from this immortal realm.

Whatever you do, allow it to come from that great love.
Whatever you think, let there be love.

Gurumayi Chidvilāsānanda

*W*hen you receive *prasād*, you extend both hands. You never receive with one hand anything that has been blessed, and you never try to snatch it away. You always put both your hands forward.

It is the same thing with meditation, repetition of the mantra, and receiving *śaktipāt* initiation. You cannot snatch these gifts from the Guru or from the mantra or from the path. You offer yourself wholeheartedly, you give your entire being. And that's when the greatest experience takes place.

Gurumayi Chidvilāsānanda

MAY

28

O friend, surrender the sword of the mind to the Self.
The moment you give in, everything you have been
longing for will take place.

Swami Muktānanda

*G*od will surrender himself to us
exactly as we surrender to him
and in the same degree.
Learn total surrender.

Swami Muktānanda

*T*he most wonderful thing about surrender is that you do it willingly—not because you have no other choice and you're forced to give in, not because you can't break the grip that old patterns have on you. You surrender because you want to surrender.

Pray for surrender, practice surrender—until one day, through grace, you attain the great experience.

Gurumayi Chidvilāsānanda

MAY

31

If you surrender to the Guru, the only thing to suffer will be
your shortcomings. When the river surrenders to the ocean,
it becomes the ocean. When a seed loses itself in the earth,
it multiplies and becomes a tree crowned with flowers
and fruit. Through surrender, one does not become smaller;
on the contrary, one becomes greater.

Swami Muktānanda

JUNE

A Seeker Is One Who Makes an Effort

*A*n aphorism of the *Śiva-sūtra* says:
prayatnaḥ sādhakaḥ
A seeker is one who makes an effort.

That which joins God and aspirant
into an inviolable unity
is called effort.

Swami Muktānanda

JUNE

2

*Y*oga is a highly evolved science. It is composed of a series of steps that begins with mastering the senses and culminates in the final reunion of the mind with supreme Consciousness.

Yoga is meeting and merging. *Yoga* is a concise term that expresses the vastness of the practices a seeker must perform.

Yoga is the seed, the beginning; it is also the fruit, the culmination. Yoga, when properly understood, invokes the experience that lies far beyond the borders of your familiar world.

Yoga is discipline, not in the sense of being crushed under a boulder that is rolling down a mountain, but of being in the presence of the Seer within.

Yoga is to know the Knower, to know the Witness, to know the One who watches your waking state, your dream state, and your state of meditation.

To know this Knower is yoga.

Gurumayi Chidvilāsānanda

JUNE

3

*Y*ou must make a strong and earnest effort
to keep your mind engaged with God all the time.
Self-realization comes through strong effort.

God resides in everyone equally.
He showers his grace on everyone equally.
His Śakti dwells in everyone equally.

How we imbibe it is up to us.

Swami Muktānanda

A true seeker is one who never slackens in his efforts. An effort, a practice, is not a mere exercise. It is the Lord himself.

When people ask, "Why must we perform the practices? Why do *sādhanā?*" the only answer is: The practices are the body of God. They are his visible form; they are vibrant with Śakti.

If you hold on to this visible aspect of God, then you're able to receive the invisible aspect; you're able to experience the *ātman,* the great Spirit.

Gurumayi Chidvilāsānanda

JUNE

5

The Muṇḍaka Upaniṣad says:
   The ātman _can always be won by truth, self-discipline, knowledge,_
   and by a life of purity.

These qualities portray the nature of _sādhanā_. They summon the
drive to follow spiritual practices.

Sādhanā, spiritual practice, has a way of creating a boundaryless
boundary to hold the experience of the Infinite.

When you have discipline, you can experience ecstasy without
allowing it to dissipate.

Gurumayi Chidvilāsānanda

*I*f all you ever see are high mountains, how can you get excited about them? It takes valleys to bring out the grandeur of mountains. Similarly, in your life, in your *sādhanā*, you cannot expect only peak experiences. You're bound to come across valleys where the sun does not shine and there's not much room for expansion. In time, you'll come to love them too.

You have to pass through so many phases in *sādhanā*, in your spiritual practices, but with grace you'll scale the heights once again. The beauty of *sādhanā* lies in the contrast. Right effort is seeing this for yourself.

Gurumayi Chidvilāsānanda

*S*ādhanā is a very beautiful word.

In Sanskrit a single word may have many shades of meaning.
The root of *sādhanā* is *sādh*, meaning "to go straight to your goal,"
and also "to submit to" or "to obey." So the word *sādhanā* means "that
which leads straight to a goal." And one who performs *sādhanā*,
the one who obeys and consents to being led, is a *sādhaka*.

Sādhaka also means one who fulfills, perfects, and completes.

Only when the spiritual journey is completed does a human
being feel fulfilled.

Gurumayi Chidvilāsānanda

JUNE

8

When I met my Guru for the first time, I was without any
worthwhile inner realization although I had practiced different
forms of yoga with devotion and discipline. But the minute I
came into his presence, Bābā Nityānanda caused something to
happen inside me. Later, he gave me a pair of wooden sandals
directly from his feet. He also spoke to me. It felt as though
with his words he had entered my inner being. Though
Muktānanda appeared the same from outside, from within
he was completely transformed.

That day I discarded the doctrine of the sufficiency of self-effort
alone. I experienced the value of the Guru's grace. Since then,
I have emphasized it to everyone. I knew sixty great teachers,
but my inner Śakti was awakened by Nityānanda alone; he
was my true Guru.

The Guru has done his work if he has awakened your inner
Śakti, but that does not mean there is no place for self-effort.

Self-effort and the Guru's grace are like the two wings of a bird:
the bird needs both to fly to the goal.

Swami Muktānanda

JUNE

9

The great sage Vasiṣṭha told Lord Rāma:

*The Truth is so close to you that you can know it
in the time it takes to blink your eyes.
Yet many ages have passed and you still have not seen it.*

If your heart were completely pure, if you had complete
faith and were completely surrendered, you would
experience the Truth immediately. But because you
do not have this kind of faith, you have to do *sādhanā*.
You have to meditate. You have to practice mantra repetition.
Only then will you be able to hold the Guru's Śakti.
Only then will you be able to assimilate his teachings.

Sādhanā is the means by which you can make your
heart pure enough and strong enough to hold the
knowledge of the Truth.

Swami Muktānanda

*T*he purer you are on the inside, the more clearly you are able to perceive the Self. When you first receive *śaktipāt*, you may have the experience of That, but to hold that experience, to become established in that experience, you have to practice for a long time. Therefore, just as you eat, drink, and do your work every day, you should also practice *sādhanā* in a disciplined manner.

The truth is that only if you practice every day, only if you combine *sādhanā* with your worldly activities, will the Guru's knowledge bear fruit for you.

Even though the Self is fully manifest within us, it is only through the awakening of the Śakti and the process of *sādhanā* that it is revealed.

Swami Muktānanda

JUNE

11

Following the spiritual path does not mean renouncing the world. To follow spiritual practices means to store as much grace within yourself as possible while living your life in this very world.

Gurumayi Chidvilāsānanda

JUNE

12

*A*ll you need for *sādhanā* is a very earnest
effort. And if you can make that earnest effort,
your *sādhanā* will go well wherever you may be.
For that, you don't have to live in an Ashram.

What you need for *sādhanā* is a burning longing
for Self-realization, and if you have that, you can
do *sādhanā* anywhere.

Swami Muktānanda

A true seeker wants to live in the state of ecstasy all the
time. He molds his whole life to make it fit for grace.

Such a seeker is ready to sacrifice all his limitations, even
the ones he likes best. He's ready to let go of the man-made
concepts of his mind. Such a seeker is disciplined because
he knows it attracts grace. Such a seeker only wants one thing:
to please the heart of God.

Gurumayi Chidvilāsānanda

JUNE

14

*E*very day God creates a new challenge for the joy of one who loves him. Such a lover of God never undermines these divine surprises. He knows that whatever God sends his way is meant to turn him into a perfect offering.

Gurumayi Chidvilāsānanda

JUNE

15

If you have the awareness that everything is God's, then you won't have to enter into a cave like a mouse to attain *samādhi*. You will attain *samādhi* right here and now.

If you consider that every job is a mode of worshiping God, then you'll attain God even while you're sweeping the floor; you'll attain God even while you're washing clothes.

Swami Muktānanda

JUNE

16

The Śvetāśvatara Upaniṣad says:
Just as a mirror covered with dust
shines brightly after it has been cleaned,
in the same way, once an embodied soul
has seen the true nature of the Self,
he becomes complete, fulfilled,
and free from sorrow.

Complete, fulfilled, and free from sorrow.
We do the practices for this attainment —
to experience the perfection within.

Gurumayi Chidvilāsānanda

This is how *sādhanā* is: the more you receive, the more you want to do *sādhanā*. The fruit is given as the process takes place.

You constantly want to make a greater and greater effort.

But let me tell you, it doesn't become easier. If you think the more *sādhanā* you do, the easier it will get, you are wrong. The more *sādhanā* you do, the more difficult it gets — but it's more exciting!

Gurumayi Chidvilāsānanda

JUNE

18

*W*hy do we follow discipline? To give rise
to the great love that exists within all of us.
With the help of discipline you become more
and more worthy of receiving grace. Very naturally
you begin to protect your inner light, to strengthen
your mind, to strengthen your heart, to strengthen
your body, to strengthen your soul. You protect
your inner light, and then the inner Self is pleased
with you and reveals itself to you. You attain a state
of equanimity that cannot be shaken.

Gurumayi Chidvilāsānanda

*T*itikṣā, forbearance, is a form of willingness.

The *Viveka-cūḍāmaṇi* defines it very practically, saying:
> To endure all kinds of afflictions without rebellion, complaint,
> or lament is called titikṣā, or forbearance.

Titikṣā is what tells you, "Don't lose hope. Nothing is ever lost.
This, too, shall pass." Like a good friend, *titikṣā* gives you the
strength to continue on the path and not become disheartened.
Again and again, it strengthens your ability to meet hard times
with the same readiness as good times.

Understand, this state of even-mindedness, this state of
forbearance, is not becoming like a brick or a piece of wood.
There is a lot of energy moving through your body. This energy
brings great vivaciousness, great enthusiasm for life, and it
removes the negative energies that compel you to perform
wrong actions.

Never give up your practices. Cultivate *titikṣā*, the inexhaustible
treasure of endurance.

Gurumayi Chidvilāsānanda

Whatever action you performed in the past becomes your destiny now. Whatever action you perform now becomes your destiny in the future.

Destiny is made by one's own endeavor, by one's own actions. Whatever kind of effort we put forth now will determine our future destiny. Therefore, effort is more important than destiny for Self-realization.

Swami Muktānanda

JUNE

21

*I*t is your destiny that brings you to the Guru to receive
śaktipāt, but then you must make the right self-effort to
cultivate the golden virtues. With this partnership, you
conserve the energy that has been awakened within you
so that it can transmute all your inferior qualities into
sublime ones.

Gurumayi Chidvilāsānanda

Nothing comes easily. Some people *do* have a good destiny. It seems that everything comes to them very easily. But understand they worked very hard for it in some other lifetime.

So there is no need to become jealous or envious of others. You shouldn't feel, "I am going through such a hard time, and everybody else is getting it so easily." The crux of the matter is, nothing great comes easily. You have to work for it; you have to put forth effort. It is as simple as that. You must make the effort.

Gurumayi Chidvilāsānanda

*Y*our will is very strong; it has a lot of power.
If you do not want to do something, do not do it.
If you do not want to think about something,
do not think about it.

Continue to put forth self-effort.
Fill yourself with positive feelings.
Think well. Pray to God.

Swami Muktānanda

JUNE

24

*B*efore time, in time, and beyond time,
I pray that I may always be grateful
to my Guru, Bābā Muktānanda.
His grace gives me sight.
His grace gives me perception.
His grace allows me to feel God's radiance,
generosity, kindness, love,
and all that the great Lord stands for.
May I continually remember
that without his grace, nothing is possible.

I offer my salutations at the feet of Bābā Muktānanda
as a continuous reminder to myself
that my body, mind, and heart belong to him.

I offer my salutations at the feet of Bābā Muktānanda
with the awareness that without his love, there is no life.

Gurumayi Chidvilāsānanda

*O*ne's whole life should become *sādhanā*, spiritual pursuit.

The goal of *sādhanā* is the inner Self, the spirit within. Through *sādhanā*, what you attain in the end is all-pervasive Consciousness. If you could maintain Consciousness while acting in the world, that would be a very good *sādhanā*.

Be aware of this: "Whatever I am doing, I am doing for the sake of inner Consciousness. I am alive for inner Consciousness." Over and over again, make yourself aware of this: "My eyes are seeing just for the sake of Consciousness. I am eating food regularly just to please Consciousness. My breath is moving in and out just for the sake of Consciousness."

This kind of understanding is called knowledge.

Just as the bubbles that arise from the ocean and merge back into it *are* the ocean, in the same way, we are all bubbles arising from Consciousness. We exist in Consciousness, and we merge back into it. We are that Consciousness. This is called *sādhanā*.

Swami Muktānanda

*T*he texture of striving, the texture of *tapasyā* is very soft. On the outside it may seem very hard, but the fabric of *tapasyā* is very, very delicate.

The physical appearance of the inner effort too may seem very strenuous, but this is misleading. It is like a lotus, which appears to have a very substantial form but is actually composed of a fine web of filaments — or like the human body, which looks as solid as a potato or a block of wood but is actually a whole world of caverns and bloodstreams and delicately connected tissues. And even subtler than that is the energy, supreme Consciousness. Striving for the Truth is as subtle and as finely textured as this.

So the texture of striving has to be extremely gentle. And this is where the knowledge of the Self, the wisdom of the Heart, comes in.

The only way striving acquires this gentle texture is through complete faith.

Gurumayi Chidvilāsānanda

JUNE

27

Sometimes people ask, "Do you think I'll make it?"

Have faith in yourself. Yes, you will make it. Why shouldn't you make it? Did somebody sign a certificate saying you will never make it? Surely you can make it. You will make it.

One of the things you have to remember is, if God has given birth to you, then that is a sure sign you can make it. He has sent you to this world with so much faith.

So, if you can have even a little bit of that faith, you will reach the goal.

Gurumayi Chidvilāsānanda

J U N E
28

A person should put forth great self-effort. A person should have a lot of enthusiasm. There is a saying: "If you look at poison all the time with good feelings, then even that poison can turn into nectar. If you look at an enemy with the awareness of a friend, then even he becomes a friend."

A person should be very strong about his purpose, his destination. He should be completely determined. And he should be enthusiastic while putting forth his own self-effort. He should think: "I will do it. I will complete it. I am going to make it."

Swami Muktānanda

JUNE

29

*W*hile you do *sādhanā*, you try to relive the ecstasy in every moment. And if there is a moment when you don't feel the ecstasy of your meditation or your chanting, then you pause. The instant you rest in this moment, you experience ecstasy. Then you gather up the particles of ecstasy and move on.

If there comes a time once again when you're not experiencing the ecstasy of meditation, of chanting, of your *sādhanā*, you pause, and you rest in this moment. Then the memories come flooding in — the memories of ecstasy. Then you move on. This is the way to do *sādhanā*.

Gurumayi Chidvilāsānanda

JUNE

30

O dear one,
  give up your pettiness and insignificance.
  Become established, right now,
  in the yoga of perfection.
  Never let sloth mar your practice.
  Our Self, Consciousness,
  is beyond the beyond.
  God and Self are one and the same.
  Through the practice of yoga, dear brother,
  the soul unites with the Self.

  Swami Muktānanda

JULY

***

Knowledge Is True Nourishment:
Resolve to Learn the Truth

JULY

1

The *Śiva-sūtra* says:
jñānam annam
Knowledge is food.

Food is the very life of the embodied soul.
By food the body arises;
by food it is sustained;
into food it merges in the end—
the earth is rich with food.

The food that is nourishing to a yogi
and brings him satisfaction and bliss
is the awareness of his own nature.

Swami Muktānanda

JULY

2

*T*he knowledge of his own true nature
is the source of a yogi's contentment.

Swami Muktānanda

*W*hy does a seeker look for a spiritual path? Why does a seeker come to a Guru? Why does a seeker search for an Ashram? *Jñānam annam* — for true nourishment, the nourishment of knowledge.

So many people feel physically weak; still, they continue to function. So many people feel weak emotionally, and still they can function. But when you feel weak in your soul, you can hardly stand up, you can barely breathe properly. If the soul feels weak, there is no life in you at all.

Jñānam annam — knowledge is the true nourishment, the true food.

Gurumayi Chidvilāsānanda

JULY

4

When you attain pure knowledge,
ignorance never troubles you again.
You pervade the entire cosmos.

Your freedom accomplishes everything.

Swami Muktānanda

JULY

5
—

*K*nowledge is the true giver of light.
It makes trust, faith, and strength flourish.
When it shines in the mind and intellect,
the Lord of the universe is beheld everywhere.

Swami Muktānanda

JULY

6

The night sky reveals all the stars and bright
planets. It gives you a glimpse of life in the universe.
Everyone looks at it and wonders, "Is there life
on those planets? Are there beings like us there?"
It's a mystery. However, your own life is an
even greater mystery.

Life in this world is a great mystery, and each
person must solve it for himself. For life to be
worthwhile, you must make the effort to find
out the greater purpose of your own existence.

Gurumayi Chidvilāsānanda

JULY

7

The fruit of self-inquiry
is merging in the supreme light.

Are you ready to begin?

Gurumayi Chidvilāsānanda

*I*t is said there are two kinds of knowledge. One, the outer knowledge, implies forgetfulness of one's nature, ignorance of inner realities, the ego-sense of "I" and "mine." The other kind of knowledge is that of unity. It arises by the grace of the Guru.

This knowledge transcends the imaginary distinctions of logic: matter and Consciousness, one Soul and many souls, the individual and the universal, the atom and the cosmos, liberation and bondage. This knowledge takes one beyond the reach of death, time, and limitation, to the supreme Self and supreme contentment.

True knowledge, then, is food in the sense that it gives perfect satisfaction and perfect rest.

Swami Muktānanda

JULY

9

A common way to understand truth is to ask what is correct and what is incorrect, what is true and what is false, what is right and what is wrong.

There is only one Truth, however, and that is God. When you look into your heart, that's what you perceive.

So make this your practice — to see God in everything and everyone, to see God's hand in your destiny.

Gurumayi Chidvilāsānanda

*T*here is only one way to attain higher knowledge, the
knowledge of supreme Consciousness, which we call God.
In fact, there is only one way to attain anything of meaning,
and that is to turn within to the stillness of the soul. This is
the message of all the saints from all cultures and traditions.
The simple truth is that nothing else will work. You have to
turn within.

So slow down and look inside.

Gurumayi Chidvilāsānanda

*P*lunge within. There lies your true kingdom.

You are the emperor of transcendental realms.

Rise above the illusion of differences. Acquire the vision
of oneness, of sages, seers, and other enlightened beings —
the vision of pure knowledge, the vision of the divine play.

Swami Muktānanda

*E*ven though the teachings are many and every tradition has its scriptures, even though there are many great teachers who are able to guide a seeker along the path, very few people actually become established in the Truth. Why? The most crucial thing for a seeker is to assimilate the teachings. Nobody else can do it for you. *You* have to assimilate the teachings.

That is why, whenever he presented the teachings, Bābā Muktānanda always emphasized one thing more than anything else. He would say: *ātmasāt karo* — "Imbibe it. Take it to heart."

Gurumayi Chidvilāsānanda

JULY

13

---

*P*ractice the teachings. That's when you become established in them.

Through the practice of the teachings, you build a temple within yourself that is so sacred that no matter what comes in contact with it, that too becomes holy.

Gurumayi Chidvilāsānanda

The scriptures capture the indescribable so beautifully,
because whatever the sages say comes straight from
their own inner experience. This is why their words
are wisdom — their words are completely baked in
the fire of their experiences.

When you hear such wisdom, it is food for the soul.

Gurumayi Chidvilāsānanda

We need the support of the words of great beings. It is through the support of their words that we are able to reflect on the abstract and then experience the Truth within ourselves.

Gurumayi Chidvilāsānanda

*T*he Upaniṣads say:

> *Where there is no darkness, nor night nor day, nor being nor*
> *nonbeing, there is the auspicious One alone, absolute and*
> *eternal. There is the glorious splendor of that light, from whom*
> *in the beginning sprang the ancient wisdom.*

The inner light is the goal. God is the goal. Wisdom is the goal. What truly lives on? Wisdom.

A beautiful landscape, if unattended, goes back to dust. A great mansion one day will fall down, either through an earthquake or through the mere passage of time. Beauty will age. The body will die. Anything you can think of—one day it will be destroyed. Nothing is going to last forever. Everything is temporary.

One thing, however, will last: that is wisdom.

Wisdom will live on.

For thousands of years wisdom has survived. To this day we say, "Two thousand years ago, three thousand years ago, the ancient sages said . . ."

This wisdom is God. This wisdom is light.

Gurumayi Chidvilāsānanda

If the nature of the inner Self is knowledge, why do we not immediately perceive the Self? Our inner Self is undecaying, perfect, eternal, and self-effulgent. Then why are we in such a plight? Why have we not discovered our own nature? What has rendered the ever-enlightened ignorant, Consciousness matter, the perfect imperfect, and the blissful miserable?

The cause of all this is ignorance. Because of our own ignorance, we have shrunk from sublimity to pettiness, from infinity to finitude, from wholeness to fragmentation. When our ignorance is completely eradicated, we become fully enlightened.

Swami Muktānanda

JULY

18

*I*gnorance is the root cause of all suffering. But when we know subjective truth and objective truth, we rise above suffering. Then we know that there is only one Truth: both the subject and the object, the seer and the seen, are one and the same.

When I see you, I am the seer and you are the seen. When you see me, you are the seer and I am the seen. When you experience the Truth, you realize there is no difference between the seer and the seen; in fact, they are one and the same.

Gurumayi Chidvilāsānanda

JULY

19

O friend, knowledge grants wisdom,
light, joy, and peace.
Everything is revealed
through this understanding.
Practice the awareness of equality,
and it will keep increasing.

Swami Muktānanda

*T*he Vedas, the ancient scriptures, do not agonize about why human beings suffer. They approach suffering very realistically. They accept that there is suffering, there is sorrow, but they want to overcome it either by recapturing the happiness that has been lost or by transcending the human condition entirely. For them the fact that there is ignorance, that reality has a dark side, only means the light is missing.

When the light of God, the light of the Truth, strikes the darkness, then darkness disappears.

Gurumayi Chidvilāsānanda

*J*ust as night can be ended by day alone, cold by heat, and sins by virtuous deeds, so ignorance can be destroyed only by knowledge.

Japa, austerities, fasting, sacrifices, and other rituals cannot dispel ignorance completely. It is knowledge that fully reveals the nature of God.

The light of the soul is indeed the light of knowledge.

Swami Muktānanda

JULY

22

In this day and age, understanding about the nature of Truth is
almost extinct. We have to turn to the pages of the scriptures
to discover once again what Truth is all about.

Truth is more than just being honest. It is more than not telling
lies, more than being open with others. Truth is recognizing the
great light that exists in everyone at all times, in all places.

In Siddha Meditation, the light of the Truth is kindled by the
Master, and you learn to perceive the world through its radiance.
The more you meditate and imbibe the teachings, the more you're
able to perceive this light expanding and blazing more brightly.
Finally, it fills every moment of your life, every corner of your life.

This is not just fantasy; it is something that actually happens after
you receive initiation.

Gurumayi Chidvilāsānanda

JULY

23

*O*nce you receive the grace of the Master,
resolve to learn the Truth from him.

Gurumayi Chidvilāsānanda

*O*ne of the verses of the *Guru-gītā* says:

> *Salutations to Śrī Guru, who with the collyrium stick of knowledge opens the eyes of one who is blinded by the darkness of ignorance.*

A person may have eyes, yet without knowledge one is considered to be spiritually blind. By applying the lotion of awareness of the inner Self, the Guru opens the inner eye of the disciple and drives away the darkness of ignorance.

Salutations to him!

Swami Muktānanda

JULY

25

Can you be awakened?
Can you drink the nectar of your own love?

With the knowledge of That,
can you laugh joyfully day and night
within yourself?
Can you recognize your own Self
in millions of forms?

If you can do this,
you are truly alive!

Swami Muktānanda

*K*ashmir Shaivism speaks about the experience of the Truth as *unmeṣa*, a flashing forth. In a split second you perceive it. Within a moment, you realize it.

Let the Truth flash forth and then hold on to it and contemplate it. In this way, instead of living in your mental projections, you will learn to live in the experiences of the Truth, the Truth that is *unmeṣa*, that flashes forth here and there: in the laughter of a child, in the noise of a machine, in the sound of footsteps, or as you watch a bird flying through the sky. It doesn't matter where or when *unmeṣa* happens; the Truth, the light of the Self, will shine forth.

Hold on to it. In it, great strength exists. In it, wonderful understanding exists. Learn to hold on to the flashes of the Truth, the light of the Self.

As you begin to experience the Truth in every grain of food, as you begin to experience it in every word, in every action, slowly but surely you become more and more established in this experience.

Gurumayi Chidvilāsānanda

JULY

27

There is a center of sublime knowledge
within every human being,
and when you enter that place,
you turn into a great poet —
you don't have to learn the art of poetry.

Swami Muktānanda

*I*f there is one thing you should never lose in your life, it is the *darśan* of the Truth. Even if you have had just a glimpse, cherish it. Don't let it go to waste.

People say, "I saw the Blue Pearl in my meditation," or "I saw the Blue Pearl in the supermarket! It flashed before my eyes, but then, I didn't experience great bliss. I didn't experience great love."

When you have the *darśan* of the inner Truth, even if you don't have a surge of emotions, it's all right. That you had the *darśan* for a moment is enough. Cherish it.

Gurumayi Chidvilāsānanda

When the sun rises, all the stars fade away in its brilliance.
Similarly, when the sun of knowledge rises in the heart and
a person experiences the essence of the Self, the universe of
diversity with its countless beings and objects is dissolved
for him. Duality perishes. The radiant sun of the Self blazes
in his eyes. Its flame radiates through every pore of his body.
As it flashes, his entire body is filled with the nectar of love.

Swami Muktānanda

The state of enlightenment devours the illusory differences that previously obsessed the yogi's concepts of death and life, matter and Consciousness, creature and creator, body and soul, man and woman, householder and renunciant.

So ignorance, too, is the food of a yogi.

Swami Muktānanda

JULY

31

The Self is eternal; it is pure and blissful. You must keep that goal in mind when you are walking the path.

When you are seeking the Truth, you have to know what the Truth is; you cannot be hazy about it, you cannot be unclear about it. You have to know. You have to know it either from the wisdom of the scriptures or from the wisdom of the great Masters — the wisdom of those people who have attained the Truth. Believe in their experience, in what they have attained, so you have that clear picture of the Truth.

And then, with that as your goal, you proceed on the path.

Gurumayi Chidvilāsānanda

AUGUST

Knowledge Is True Nourishment:
Receive the Teachings from a Master

AUGUST

1

*W*ho am I? What am I? From time immemorial this one question has bewildered anyone who wants to know the Truth, who wants to know life in its fullness.

Who am I? What am I? A person may search through all the universes, inner and outer, for years on end trying to trace this question back to its source.

Who am I? What am I? No answer that he finds on his own will hit the mark. None of them will be able to satisfy him completely.

Who am I? What am I? This is the question. And this is the quest that gave birth to the lineage of Masters and disciples. At some point every seeker comes to understand that he must find someone who has solved the magnificent riddle and who lives in the experience of the answer. Not someone who *has* the answer, but someone who lives in the experience of the answer.

Gurumayi Chidvilāsānanda

AUGUST

2

*O*nce a seeker is seized with a
longing to know his true nature,
the only way he will ever receive a
convincing answer is by becoming
the disciple of a true Master.

Gurumayi Chidvilāsānanda

AUGUST

3

---

*T*here is only one way shown by the Guru — the way
of *śaktipāt*, the way of grace, of compassion.

When a seeker is blessed by the Guru, a new spiritual body
is created inside him and he begins to move through different
worlds. The Guru's Śakti works within him, and the disciple
receives currents of new inspiration and knowledge; his
mind is totally cleansed.

Swami Muktānanda

AUGUST

4

This is the science of Gurus and disciples.

When you hear something from the Guru, all you need is one word—because everything is inside us. You don't need anything from outside.

Every day we see That, but still we don't have knowledge. Every day we hear about That, but still we don't understand. We are surrounded by that divine pure knowledge, we are in the midst of it, but still we are not aware. Inside us and outside us, above and below us, behind us and in front of us, that Consciousness is all-pervasive. Consciousness is just like the ocean, and we are all the waves and ripples of that ocean.

You don't have to worry about anything; you don't have to search for that Truth anywhere else. Through the grace of the Guru, through the love of the Guru, your real eye will open.

Swami Muktānanda

First, you find a Master who is true
and can give you enlightenment,
and then, you become completely
one-pointed on the Guru's teachings.

A disciple who receives the teachings
receives everything.

Gurumayi Chidvilāsānanda

AUGUST

6

*B*elieve in the Guru's grace
and allow the experience
of the Absolute to emerge.

Gurumayi Chidvilāsānanda

In the *Guru-gītā*, Lord Śiva instructs Pārvatī:

One should purify one's mind by following the path shown by the Guru. Whatever transient things are ascribed to the Self should be discarded.

This verse is very powerful.

You don't need to go anywhere to purify yourself. If you can only submerge your restless mind in the teachings of the Guru, it will be cleansed; it will shine with the Guru's great wisdom.

Gurumayi Chidvilāsānanda

AUGUST

8

$\mathcal{W}$hen devotion to the Master becomes steady,
the wisdom of the Master automatically descends
into the disciple.

Gurumayi Chidvilāsānanda

AUGUST

9

Through the Guru's grace realize the divinity, the omniscience, dwelling within your heart. Experience that profound inner peace.

Acquire the inner eye of knowledge by which you can clearly see the whole world within. You will be able to see the entire cosmos while sitting in one place.

Swami Muktānanda

AUGUST

10

*F*rom stillness, everything springs forth.

In the depth of your being, great serenity is found.
Divine wisdom is imparted in the silence of the
innermost heart.

Anyone who wishes to experience true ecstasy must
extract it from the depth of his own heart.

Gurumayi Chidvilāsānanda

AUGUST

11

*B*oth matter and Consciousness arise from silence, the silence
of God, the silence of light. The same profound silence exists
in minerals, plants, and oceans. It also exists at the core of every
living being. From silence comes all growth and development.
It is here, in silence, that the search for knowledge culminates.
When you become immersed in the stillness of your soul, you
understand everything.

Gurumayi Chidvilāsānanda

In the *Guru-gītā*, Pārvatī, the great Śakti, asks her beloved
Lord Śiva:

> *O God, O Lord of gods, O higher than the highest, O teacher of*
> *the universe, O benevolent one, O great God, initiate me into the*
> *knowledge of the Guru. O Lord, by which path can an embodied soul*
> *become one with Brahman, the absolute Reality? Have compassion*
> *on me, O Lord! I bow to your feet.*

These questions that come in the form of requests set the tone
for the unfolding of the mystery of the Guru. You can feel how
deep the Goddess's yearning is. You can sense the urgency of her
quest for knowledge. You can feel the pull to know the Truth.
You can actually experience the quality of perfect surrender in
her voice. She appeals to the Lord, not out of pride, but with the
pure longing of a true disciple. It is this that moves Lord Śiva to
disclose the mystery of the Guru. The humility and longing
of Pārvatī draw grace from the depth of his cosmic Heart. Then
knowledge springs from the fountain of his being in the form
of the *Guru-gītā*, and all humankind is uplifted.

Gurumayi Chidvilāsānanda

AUGUST

13

Although the scriptures emphasize surrender, vows, and discipline, one does not really have to surrender to them—one can interpret them in any way one likes.

But one cannot interpret the Guru.

Swami Muktānanda

AUGUST

14

*Y*ou may change the scriptures, but the Guru will certainly change you. He will begin by awakening you, by telling you that you have forgotten your own Self. Lacking knowledge of your Self, you are deep in the sleep of ignorance. The Guru will open your eyes to your darkness, ignorance, and forgetfulness. Only after knowing darkness is it possible to find light. Only one who falls can get up. Unless a seeker knows what it is to fall down, it is difficult for him to rise.

After the Guru has made you aware of your condition, he will give you the vision of your own Self.

Swami Muktānanda

*W*hen I went to Gaṇeśpurī and met Nityānanda Bābā,
the supreme *avadhūt*, I was overjoyed. No — I was fulfilled.
After a bath in the hot springs, I went for his *darśan*. He was
poised in a simple, easy posture on a plain cot, smiling gently.
His eyes were in *śāmbhavī mudrā* (eyes open but gaze directed
within). What divine luster glowed in those eyes! His body
was dark, and he was wearing a simple loincloth. He said,
"So you've come."

"Yes sir," I answered.

I stood for a while and then sat down. There I realized the
highest. I am still sitting there. Where shall I go now?

Peace cannot be had in the absence of the Guru, nor can
self-contentment or inspiration. When I obtained Sadguru
Nityānanda, I obtained all.

Swami Muktānanda

AUGUST

16

*Y*ou receive teachings from the Master in many different ways. A teaching is given to you in the form you must receive it, not in the form you *think* you must receive it.

Gurumayi Chidvilāsānanda

When the fire of knowledge is ignited in your being, the
impurities of many, many lifetimes begin to burn away.
Sometimes the Guru's fire of knowledge rages inside you.
Sometimes it cools down so much, you think it is only
embers; you wonder if it is going to die out. But it is
burning nevertheless, consuming everything that holds
you back; and then once again, it blazes. So when you
allow this fire to rage inside yourself, you attain a
greater state.

When the fire of knowledge roars through your being,
you know you have a Guru; you are not alone.

Gurumayi Chidvilāsānanda

*T*he most incredible thing about a great being is that he is able to impart wisdom, the Truth, through any form at any time. So if you are open to the teachings of the great beings, if you are open to God's love, then he can manifest through any form, any object, at any time.

If you keep yourself open, *darśan* will happen at all times. *Darśan* is always taking place. When you stop listening only to the limitations of your mind and ego, you will find yourself swimming in the ocean of Consciousness. In every word you'll experience great joy. The Truth will emanate from every person.

In Siddha Yoga, Bābā's compassion and the compassion of his Guru, Bhagavān Nityānanda, were and are tremendous. When the time is right, they grant the *darśan* of infinity. Until then we always keep ourselves prepared: prepared to experience the Truth, prepared to know the Truth, prepared to have *darśan*.

Gurumayi Chidvilāsānanda

To be a disciple doesn't mean you have to be very close to the Guru physically. You come very close to the Guru when you follow the teachings, when you take the words of the Guru to your heart.

Gurumayi Chidvilāsānanda

*B*ābā always used to say his heart soared in the sky every time he realized somebody wanted his knowledge, his wisdom.

There is such bliss in wisdom, in knowing the Truth.

Gurumayi Chidvilāsānanda

I don't want a person who can give me something.
I want a person who can imbibe what I want to give
him, through his heart.

Swami Muktānanda

AUGUST

22

True knowledge is not dry;
it releases bliss.
If it does not release bliss,
it is not knowledge.

Swami Muktānanda

*P*rayers are not just for the sake of having a wish or a desire fulfilled. You can also pray for knowledge, for the Truth.

You can pray for discrimination, for knowing what you want and what you don't want, what you really want to keep, what you really don't want to keep.

Prayer is for knowledge also.

Gurumayi Chidvilāsānanda

When you read philosophy, it will give you knowledge; when you meditate, it will give you the experience.

Philosophy and meditation are like reading a cookbook and baking a cake. In reading the cookbook, you learn how to prepare a cake, but just by reading alone, you are not going to be satisfied. You have to bake the cake and eat it also.

Today, people only read cookbooks, but they don't actually make the cakes. They just read about them, and that's why they are so hungry.

It's fine to read philosophy, but to attain what philosophy is speaking about, you have to meditate.

In meditation you have the experience of That.

Swami Muktānanda

*F*ull knowledge, supreme bliss, perfection —
all arise through meditation.
Muktānanda,
only by meditation
does the knowledge gained from the scriptures
become a living experience.

Swami Muktānanda

AUGUST

26

When you practice the teachings,
you experience the Consciousness
that resides in their words.

Gurumayi Chidvilāsānanda

The whole world should be revealed to a person
as different parts of his own body.
This is knowledge that only the Guru can give.
The entire universe is your own body;
your body is the entire universe.

Gurumayi Chidvilāsānanda

AUGUST

28

When the Guru's knowledge arises
from within, you see the play
of the Self everywhere.

Swami Muktānanda

Self-inquiry and study are not just a matter of memorizing a book, after all, but of allowing your inner knowledge to flower.

Sometimes performing self-inquiry, looking deeply into the nature of your Self, may feel like banging on the door to the soul. At other times, it may feel like a cry from the depths of your soul. However, depending on the strength of self-inquiry and its intensity, its urgency, this practice alone may be enough to fling open the gates of liberation.

Gurumayi Chidvilāsānanda

*W*hen you are engaged in *svādhyāya*, study of the Self, your
gratitude doubles every second. This inner work — the study
of your own true nature — frees you from the habit of blaming
others for your condition in life. This inner study creates a
haven that gives you the power to overcome your faults.

Knowing the great Self is the secret of supreme peace. Gratitude
for such a state shimmers like a billion stars in the night sky.

Gurumayi Chidvilāsānanda

*I*t is always nice to be reminded of the Truth. Never feel you know so much that you don't need anyone to remind you of anything.

Keep yourself open. Teachings come from everything: from a small ant to a great elephant. So remain open to knowledge all the time.

Gurumayi Chidvilāsānanda

SEPTEMBER

✐

Where There Is Dharma, There Is Victory

SEPTEMBER

1

*D*harma is a beautiful word in the Sanskrit language. It is rich with meaning. *Dharma* literally means "that which holds together." *Dharma* also means "righteousness," "right action," or "duty."

Just to say the word *dharma* uplifts you and fills you with inspiration. It brings to mind those noble ones who have lived their lives in service of the highest principles, who have sacrificed their lives for the rest of humanity.

Through *dharma* a human being is able to transform his ordinary vision into a perception of the Divine.

Gurumayi Chidvilāsānanda

*T*he greatest duty of a human being is to know God and to worship him with love. The *Mahābhārata* says:

> *The secret of* dharma
> *is hidden in the cave of the heart.*

Dharma is the external reflection of a pristine and clear heart.

Gurumayi Chidvilāsānanda

SEPTEMBER

3

One's highest duty is to worship the Self,
the Lord who blazes in the hearts of all.

Swami Muktānanda

SEPTEMBER

4

$\mathcal{I}$f you remain true to your heart,
victory will inevitably be yours.

Gurumayi Chidvilāsānanda

There are two kinds of *dharma*: the duty to the Self, *svadharma*, which is the supreme duty, and our social or professional duties, which are secondary.

If you are a teacher, it is your duty to teach. If you are a police officer, it is your duty to see that law and order are maintained. If you are a parent, it is your sacred duty to regard your children as divine and to raise them with discipline and love. So whatever field you are in, your duty lies in that field.

There are so many different *dharmas* and forms of duty. But the most important *dharma*, which is also the most natural for a human being, is to become one with the Self, with the Being from whom we have all emerged.

This *dharma* has been sanctioned by all traditions and scriptures.

Swami Muktānanda

The fundamental message of *dharma* is this: a person should remember that everyone is a part of God.

Troubles and diseases flee from one who follows the command of God in his own heart, who incorporates God's will into his own heart, and who puts this knowledge into practice.

Swami Muktānanda

*A*lways live as an example to others.

Each one must live as an example to everyone else.
You have this responsibility to your own life and to
the entire world.

Gurumayi Chidvilāsānanda

So many people say,
  "I don't know what my *dharma* is.
  I don't know what I'm supposed to do."

You exist; that's your *dharma*.
You work; that's your *dharma*.
You're loving to others; that's your *dharma*.

You keep your heart in a good state;
that's your *dharma*.
You keep your mind in a good state;
that's your *dharma*.
You help those who come to you seeking help;
that's your *dharma*.

So your *dharma* is truly to exist,
because this is the life you have received from God.

Gurumayi Chidvilāsānanda

*E*ach person has his or her own *dharma* to follow, and you
must play your own role fully. Whatever role you have chosen
to play in this world, play it to the utmost. Never quit in the
middle. Do not become disheartened. No matter what happens,
pick yourself up once again and move on. Be a warrior.

Because each one follows his or her own *dharma* — which
is different from any other *dharma*, which has its own variety,
its own novelty, its own uniqueness — this entire universe
is magnificent.

Gurumayi Chidvilāsānanda

*W*hatever a person considers valuable for himself,
he should give exactly the same thing to others, to
his society.

One should find out what is good for oneself, and
one can discover that from the examples of the great
beings. What you want to do for yourself, do for others
also. If there is a conflict between your duty to yourself
and your duty to others, that means you have become
involved in some sort of self-deception.

To want the same thing for yourself and for others,
and to help others achieve those things, is your duty
to society. You should think that you are society and
society is you. Live and act in society following the
footsteps of the great beings.

Swami Muktānanda

*E*ach individual makes an offering to his own world according to his own ability and his own worth. A person who engages in meditation as a spiritual practice allows himself to be transmuted into light. Then wherever he goes, he transforms the atmosphere around him into one that is loving and harmonious and glorifies God.

And this does happen as you continually meditate on the light of God.

Gurumayi Chidvilāsānanda

In their prayers, the sages and seers constantly expressed their utmost reverence for the Creator and his creation. To protect the supreme love in their hearts, to worship the lord of *dharma*, they lived their lives with exquisite caution. Though they had complete wisdom and were all-knowing, their reverence, even for the tip of a blade of grass, was remarkable. Their lives were steeped in humility. They walked the earth, offering their salutations to every particle of dust.

This is the way to live one's life: as a prayer, as worship.

Gurumayi Chidvilāsānanda

*H*aving the right thoughts,
in the right place,
with the right person,
while performing the right actions —
that is *dharma*.

Gurumayi Chidvilāsānanda

SEPTEMBER

14

*T*hrough the observance of *dharma*, you maintain
your greatness even in times of hardship. It is like a
storehouse. Then, just like the lighted end of a torch
that can be turned in any direction, your flame will
always point upward.

Gurumayi Chidvilāsānanda

A person should engage himself in performing good actions. He should not wonder whether they are going to bear fruit or not. In the *Bhagavad-gītā* the Lord says, "O Arjuna, keep performing good actions. Never wonder what kind of fruit you are going to attain and when."

No action will go to waste. When the right season comes, the trees blossom and bear fruit.

Swami Muktānanda

*T*he *dharma* of the wind is to blow; the *dharma* of fire is to burn. Ever since the beginning of creation, nature has followed its own *dharma*, anchored firmly in the will of God. Obedience to the will of God reveals your own *dharma*.

If you're ever feeling confused about your *dharma*, sit and watch a river. Let its steady flowing be a message. Or go to a mountain and meditate. Let its endurance, the great starkness of its peaks, inspire you. In this way, you can meditate on the workings of nature in order to learn obedience and receive teachings on *dharma*.

Gurumayi Chidvilāsānanda

Someone once said, "Gurumayi, can you give me a reason to live?" She was putting her whole being into the question.

She said, "Up to now I have had no reason to live. Please give me a reason."

I said, "The only reason *I* live is for God. So if that can be a good reason for you, then please take it. Live for God, live to do his work, to abide by his will."

She said that sounded good.

Your life is never useless. Your life is never in vain. Just that you exist proves that you are the flame of God, and God wants to shine through you. And that's why you are here in this world at this time.

Gurumayi Chidvilāsānanda

SEPTEMBER

18

---

*W*hen you put *dharma* before everything else and let God's love take charge of your life, every moment shines with brilliance.

Only a life that rests in God's hands can fulfill its purpose and its promise. Such a life is full of peace.

Gurumayi Chidvilāsānanda

*D*harma, the path of duty:

When you follow your duty,
it becomes your savior.

When you follow your duty,
it becomes your protection.

When you follow your duty,
it becomes your companion.

When you protect *dharma*,
dharma protects you.

Gurumayi Chidvilāsānanda

*A*lthough every person inevitably encounters
difficulties in life,
if you courageously pursue Truth
and righteousness,
you will certainly triumph.

Swami Muktānanda

Many people call themselves workaholics. Many people
take great pride in the amount of work that they do.
They work from morning till night, from night till morning.
They work and work and work — more than a donkey,
more than a bull, more than a waterfall.

However, understand: if you just work, it has no importance.
It's when you let God work through you that your work has
great value. That's when you experience God's glory.

Gurumayi Chidvilāsānanda

Delight in your actions;
enjoy your world.
Act with utter absorption of mind and body,
and without expectation.
Consider all work
to be the worship of the Lord;
do it for his sake alone.

Swami Muktānanda

How do you know if you're doing God's will?

You should always ask God this question.
Even if you know the answer within yourself,
you should always ask God. Never forget to
converse with God.

When you go to bed at night, talk to God.
When you wake up first thing in the morning,
talk to God. If you ask God within yourself,
then you get the answer and you know what
you're doing; you truly experience his will.

So you should always keep the conversation
with God alive within yourself.

Gurumayi Chidvilāsānanda

SEPTEMBER

24

*W*hen you abandon yourself to the will of God, you feel such great devotion. You experience the strong sweetness of love. You become a true warrior on the spiritual path. Your heart is completely attached to God's heart. Your only path is the will of God.

When you abandon yourself to the will of God, you have complete determination. Yet you are not bullheaded, you are not stubborn. You must be flexible to follow the will of God.

In greatness, there is complete flexibility.

Gurumayi Chidvilāsānanda

Some people turn to service as a means of their own survival. But when you come from the experience of the inner Self, you serve to beautify God's creation. It is as if you become his, as if you work only for God—not because God could not do his work without you, but because it is sheer joy to belong to God. When you have the experience, "I am God's," then you can truly live the life that God has given to you.

When you have the feeling of belonging to God, when your heart is God's heart, you can hear the thunder of his laughter rolling inside you. You feel God's presence in your being, and the pulse of his love moves you forward on his path. If others derive joy from your service, you know it is really God they are seeing in your actions. When this is the case, your service is pure and inspired, flowing naturally and inevitably like a bud blossoming into a flower.

Gurumayi Chidvilāsānanda

SEPTEMBER

26

One who serves the Lord in his heart with great joy
serves the entire world.

Swami Muktānanda

The sages of the Vedas say:
Day and night we approach you, O Lord,
with reverential homage,
through sublime thoughts and noble deeds.

This is *dharma*.

Gurumayi Chidvilāsānanda

When you give yourself to *dharma*, it promotes love in the hearts of everyone. What people really appreciate is the way you pursue your duty. It becomes an inspiration.

No matter how beautiful you are, it's not your beauty that makes people feel great — it's how you follow your *dharma*. It doesn't matter how wealthy you are; it's not your money that inspires other people — it's how you follow your *dharma*. It doesn't matter how poor you are; it's not your poverty that moves people's hearts — it's the way you lead your life.

The *dharma* you follow is what touches people's hearts — nothing external. It's what you are inside and how you express it that has an impact, that moves everyone's soul.

Gurumayi Chidvilāsānanda

SEPTEMBER

29

*Y*ou can see the message very clearly
everywhere you look, on all sides.
It comes from the knowers of the Truth
of all traditions. They all say the same thing:
Experience God's vastness within yourself,
but also feed the hungry.
Experience God's bounty within yourself;
also, listen to the sorrowful words of your friend.
Experience God's love in your own being;
also, don't mind making your own bed
when you wake up in the morning.

Both mundane and spiritual belong to God,
so learn to share with others
the greatness you experience within yourself.

Every knower of the Truth
has brought about this harmony and balance.

Gurumayi Chidvilāsānanda

*I*f nothing else ever takes place in this world, there is one thing that will certainly happen, and that is death. Death is inevitable. The world is transitory, life is transitory.

Live your life in such a way that at the end, you don't have to worry, "Have I done the right thing? Have I performed dharmic actions? Have I fulfilled the purpose of my life?"

Live your life in such a way that when the time comes to leave this world, you don't have to worry, "Have I performed good deeds? Have I done enough charitable work? Have I thought about God enough? Will I go to heaven? What will happen to me after I die? What will happen to those who survive after I die?" Live your life in such a way that you don't have to be anxious at the end of your life.

Live your life in such a way that when the moment arrives for you to leave this world, you are totally at peace. You are happy that it is time to leave. There is nothing more to be done, nothing more to be achieved. You are simply happy.

Gurumayi Chidvilāsānanda

OCTOBER

Time Is the Absolute

OCTOBER

1

*T*ime has many facets: past, present, and future.
Yet, it is unending. When time has become totally
still inside you, knowledge arises within, and you
experience the Truth.

If you try to catch up with time, you'll never succeed;
time has to become still for you.

And this time, this eternal time, is the blissful Absolute.

Gurumayi Chidvilāsānanda

*E*ven when death occurs for this physical body, the Śakti of the Guru won't die. It will remain as it is. It will always be alive.

A river keeps flowing and one day it merges into the ocean. The river ceases to exist, but the ocean still exists. The river becomes the ocean. The river disappears — not the ocean. In the same way, *jīvātma*, the individual soul, merges into the supreme Soul, into God. So even though the individual soul ceases to exist, God still exists.

Therefore, have no worries. Whenever you want to meet him, Muktānanda will appear. Right now I am in the form of a river, and afterwards I will be the entire ocean.

Swami Muktānanda

*T*ime is God. Time is divine. Time is the lightning bolt. Time is the flow of Consciousness. When you have this sublime awareness of time, every breath you draw brings you the vision of God.

Those who do not have such vision say that time is death. Time is the messenger of sorrow. Time is a thief. Time is a killer. Time is vicious. Time is invisible. Time is dark. When you have this awareness of time, every breath you draw carries a cold blade in its folds. Every breath cuts you to the quick.

Time, like the world, is as you see it. What you give to time is what comes back to you. You must never forget that. Time is the way it is for you—depending on how you have treated time.

Time is energy. Time is God.

Gurumayi Chidvilāsānanda

*E*very moment belongs to you. Every moment is yours.
Use every moment as Brahman, as the Absolute. Let every
moment be the love of God.

Let every moment be filled with light.

When you know and experience every moment as love,
as light, you preserve your energy, you increase your luster
and enthusiasm.

You experience love in every moment.

It is not that sometime in the future you are going to
attain something great. It has never happened like that.
It is in this very moment that something great is going
to happen to you.

Gurumayi Chidvilāsānanda

$\mathcal{T}$ime is the most precious, delicate, and elusive energy there is. You cannot wait for tomorrow to do *sādhanā*, or to begin self-inquiry. You cannot be comfortable with the feeling that yesterday you did a lot of soul-searching and today you are going to rest.

Yesterday, today, and tomorrow are different folds in the fabric of eternity. The most important time, the one that is shining before you, is now. This is the time to know God—not yesterday and not tomorrow. Wake up! The sages say, "Wake up, right now! You must wake up."

Gurumayi Chidvilāsānanda

That which was not, came.
That which came must go.
Muktānanda, remain calm and steady
in the midst of all that comes and goes.

What is inevitable must happen.
You cannot prevent it.
Muktānanda, recognize the inevitable.
Remain tranquil in yourself.

This brief life passes quickly
and in the end one dies.
Now is the time, Muktānanda,
to meditate on the Self.

Swami Muktānanda

In this very body become liberated. Do not waste your time.
You never know when this body is going to fall away. This is
a simple truth the saints tell us again and again and again, but
somehow we feel we are an exception. We think God will have
so much mercy on us that we can do whatever we want; and
then when we need to know him, we'll know him. Don't take
it for granted. Don't take your life for granted, don't take your
body for granted, don't take your mind for granted.

Many times you may feel, "My mind is so strong. It can do
anything. It will always be there for me." It isn't so. Nothing
is always there for you; everything has been given to you.
Everything has a time limit: when the time is up, the time is
up. You can never borrow time.

You can borrow money from the bank, but you can never
borrow time, not even from God. Even he does not lend time.

He has given us something, and it is up to us to make good
use of it.

Gurumayi Chidvilāsānanda

*M*any of you are seeking God-realization, so a very important question arises—What God are you seeking? Is it the eternal, all-pervading Being, the One who permeates all and who is present every moment within every heart? Or is it some god who has to be discovered, who is not present within us, but is present in some distant corner of the universe?

The eternal Being is present in all times, in all spaces and all substances, and is with us every moment. If it were not so, we could not attain him.

Swami Muktānanda

The entire universe is clothed in time.
Time makes the sun rise and the night fall.
Time is the supreme decision-maker.
In time you cut teeth, in time you lose them.

Time is the witness of ignorance.
It also witnesses the merging
of the individual soul into the supreme Soul.
Nothing goes unnoticed by time.
The whole universe revolves around time.

Gurumayi Chidvilāsānanda

*D*evelop this awareness: every day is special in its own fashion.
You must be vigilant, poised for the divine moment on the
threshold of change, the moment of transition. The past is not
completely gone yet. It lies behind you, but it has no hold on
you anymore. The future is before you, approaching like a fresh
wind, and yet its features are dim and its responsibility is still
unknown. In this divine moment, you are free. This is the
eternal present, the threshold of renewal and promise. You
are buoyant with the weightlessness of the great Spirit, the
great Śakti. Your feet are touching the ground, but you feel
no gravity.

This is the moment that is divine with possibility. You're
soaring high, but you're still supported by the present instant.
The tender shoot of ecstasy is vibrating in every pore of your
being. This divine moment is priceless. It is a treasure beyond
compare. Trying to describe this moment is like trying to
capture the morning mist in a bowl.

The great ones continually live in this moment. They never
sink into *apasmāra*, the state of forgetfulness. The great ones
perceive every moment as a miracle filled with Śakti, filled
with grace.

Gurumayi Chidvilāsānanda

What is the purpose of a human life? To know God, to know the Truth. There is no doubt about this. One of the scriptures of India says:

All the wealth of the universe cannot purchase even a moment of life.
If a person wastes his precious life, his mistake is unforgivable.

This is a strong and wonderful statement. If you waste your time, it's very difficult to be forgiven. The sages imparted their teachings, their knowledge, without wasting time or words; they always went straight to the point. They said: Know the Truth. There is no time to lose. Your life is precious.

Gurumayi Chidvilāsānanda

The man who sees time as God
does all his work on time.
Muktānanda, time is infinitely valuable.
Time is lost only in time.
Once gone, it cannot be recovered.

You can give everything to others,
but do not give them your time.
Muktānanda, see God standing between
two instants of wasted time.

Swami Muktānanda

*O*ne of the ways to respect time is through meditation, through the remembrance of God. In fact, in many traditions you remember God at the beginning of each segment of time.

You remember God in the early morning, before the day begins. You remember God at noontime, before the afternoon begins. You remember God in the evening, before the night comes.

So you remember God at each of these junctions of time, and by remembering God, you offer all your thoughts and all your actions to him. In this way you respect time; you recognize that time is divine, time is God.

Time does not exist only for you to indulge in sense pleasures. Time, too, wants to be uplifted by your actions. It wants to be glorified by your presence on this planet.

Gurumayi Chidvilāsānanda

OCTOBER

14

We desire to make the impossible possible.

This world is like a boarding house or a hotel in which we are temporary guests. Trying to find eternity in the things of the world is like trying to stop a river whose very nature is to flow.

Swami Muktānanda

If you don't think every moment is filled with ambrosia, you haven't seen Śiva's play. You haven't worshiped him in the form of the moment — as time, as infinity, and as the eternal sphere, the eternal space.

Gurumayi Chidvilāsānanda

There is a gap between one thought and another. Have you ever thought about the stillness and stability that exist in the space between two thoughts?

That is the Self. That is God. That is the Truth. That is Self-realization.

Swami Muktānanda

In his *Amṛtānubhava*, "The Nectar of Self-Awareness," the great poet-saint Jñāneśvar Mahārāj wrote:

The natural state of the Self is found at the invisible juncture, the timeless moment between the fading of the seer and the seen and their reappearance. It is like that wavering moment when sleep has just ended, but we have not yet fully awakened.

The state of the inner Self is in every moment, and the experience of it can be seized at the invisible juncture — between two thoughts, for example. As one thought dissolves and another thought arises, there is always a short interval, a space, and this is a timeless moment.

Gurumayi Chidvilāsānanda

So close is the Truth.

As the breath comes in, it stops for a second within. Find that place. As the breath goes out, it stops for a fraction of a moment. Find that place. Where does it dissolve?

When pain arises in the body, from where does it arise? When it goes away, where does it really go? Where does laughter come from? When you finish laughing, where does it go?

As you focus on the point within where the breath dissolves, you lose yourself in it. As you breathe out, the same thing takes place — you are lost for a second.

In this inner space and in this outer space, there is supreme bliss. Because of this space, even when we're in pain, joy lingers on. This space makes it possible for us to live.

The awakened Śakti magnifies the experience.

Gurumayi Chidvilāsānanda

*A*s the breath comes in and goes out, it makes a sound. When it comes in, it makes the sound *ham*, and when it goes out, it makes the sound *saḥ*. The sound of the breath coming in and going out is the repetition of the *haṁsa* mantra.

When the breath comes in with the sound *ham* and merges inside, there is a fraction of a moment that is completely still and free of thought. When the breath goes out with the sound *saḥ* and merges outside, the same moment exists there also. This is the *madhya-daśā*, the space between the breaths.

Sit very quietly. Become aware of the breath coming in and going out, repeating *haṁsa, haṁsa*. Understand that *ham* is the perfect "I," the pure Consciousness. Understand that *saḥ* is the universal energy. Focus subtly on the place where these syllables arise and subside, and you will know the Self. This is the true state of God. You are That.

Swami Muktānanda

*I*t is very difficult for people to believe in ecstasy. But when you find the space that exists inside and outside — the timeless time, the pointless point — and when it becomes a prolonged space inside and outside, ecstasy is no longer a concept: it is the experience.

In the beginning, it's a practice to find this place inside where the breath dissolves before it arises, and outside where the breath dissolves before it arises again. But later on, you can get in touch with it whenever you want it, because you know where it is. It has become your own experience. You don't have to go looking for it; it's just there.

Gurumayi Chidvilāsānanda

*T*ime is very important. In the words of the poet-saint Sundardās:

Time both creates and dissolves.
It seizes us and reduces us to ashes.
It is time that makes us move and walk,
but only in order to lead us astray.
Time summons us and makes us great.
It draws us to the forest
or to the banks of a river.
Sundardās says,
time will vanish as soon as we realize the Self.

As soon as you recognize the stillness of the soul, you are no longer afraid of time. Time becomes timeless. And in the fleeting moments of your life, you experience eternity.

Gurumayi Chidvilāsānanda

$\mathcal{Y}$ou are the blissful Self.
Throughout past, present, and future,
you remain independent.
You are immortal, eternal, without relationship.
You are never dependent.
You are supreme, all-pervasive, immovable.
None but you exists.
You alone are Truth.

You surpass both matter and light.
You are nondual, supreme.
You are the quintessence of eternity.
You are *oṁ*, the foundation of all,
transcending *māyā* and the world.

O seeker,
hear the immortal voice of the Self, and wake up!
Balanced and serene in the world, pursue yoga.

Swami Muktānanda

OCTOBER

23

Seize hold of the moment that is before you and begin
again your journey to the inner universe. Right now,
wherever you are on the path, however many times you
have faltered, begin again.

There is such joy in beginning the day anew. Just as your
breath travels in and out over and over again, tirelessly,
in the same way, if you feel you have faltered on the path,
begin once again.

Gurumayi Chidvilāsānanda

*B*ecome new from the inside out. With this newness, there is an incredible yearning to know your own Self, to experience tranquility, to merge into the inner Self. A person who maintains newness glows with a noticeable light.

Your attainment of spirituality does not come from how many years you've been on the spiritual path. Your attainment comes from how new you've made yourself as time has passed by.

Gurumayi Chidvilāsānanda

A human life is precious. Most people only understand its value when they think they are going to lose it. But the sages say, "Wake up now!"

Understand your life is precious right now. Don't wait for a drama to take place before you understand that your body is a temple of God, your house holds the light of God, you are a vehicle of the great Truth.

Gurumayi Chidvilāsānanda

*O*nce you experience the great, blazing energy within yourself, you'll come to love every second of your life. Instead of dwelling on the past or escaping into the future, you'll love the very moment in which you exist.

Gurumayi Chidvilāsānanda

*I*t has taken you lifetimes to come into the presence of your own inner Self in the form of the Guru.

Now that you have arrived, take great care to be present.

Gurumayi Chidvilāsānanda

OCTOBER

28

*W*hen the great love invites you, go. Never falter. Never hold yourself back. As the sages have always said, if you hold yourself back, one day you will repent, because time doesn't wait for you. You may wait for the time to come again, but time is merciless. It doesn't stop. It moves on. So at a time when this great love asks you to come — go!

Do not doubt whether the way will be filled with difficulties and hardships — just follow.

When this great love speaks to you, listen; follow its command. Give yourself to the awakening of this love. And if its voice within you threatens to shatter all your concepts, let them go — don't hold yourself back.

Gurumayi Chidvilāsānanda

*T*he supreme Self," the *Mahārthamañjarī* says, "is eternal, permanent. It appears impermanent only in relation to the destruction of the moment."

For an ordinary person, a moment is destroyed; time has duality. A happy moment is finished and an unhappy moment comes. A good time ends and a bad time takes over. People who live in this state of constant impending doom experience the moment being destroyed.

For a sage, no moment is ever destroyed. Each moment is infinite. Each moment merges into eternity.

Gurumayi Chidvilāsānanda

*A*s the Kuṇḍalinī fire burns away all impurities, the ultimate experience is: everything exists within this being. And when this experience takes place, you perceive time; you know the past, present, and future. There's no longer a barrier within to keep you away from the experience of time.

When this experience takes place, you're able to honor each moment of time; when this experience takes place, you're able to give yourself to time. And when you can sacrifice yourself to time, time sacrifices itself to you; and literally, without any exaggeration, time stops for you to achieve what you want to, and then it moves on. Time becomes your servant.

Then wherever you go, it is the perfect time; whatever you do, you're doing it at the perfect time; whatever you say, it is the perfect time. You are no longer the slave of time, because you become the eternal Witness; you become time itself.

Gurumayi Chidvilāsānanda

OCTOBER

31

When you perceive the inner light, it is silvery bright. As you concentrate on this silvery light that arises within you, you go beyond that light also. And then you see it is an ocean of light. You live in the ocean of light, and this is the timelessness of time. Even though it may seem that day rolls into night and night rolls into day, and the days and nights roll into the weeks and the months and the years, in this ocean of light there is everything and there is nothing. You exist, and simultaneously, you don't exist.

Live your life in the timelessness of time.

Gurumayi Chidvilāsānanda

NOVEMBER

Whatever You Give, That's What You Receive

NOVEMBER

1

*W*hatever you give,
that's what you receive,
nothing else.
This is a law of nature.

Swami Muktānanda

*I*n an important passage of the *Bhagavad-gītā*, Lord Kṛṣṇa declares, "O Arjuna, this body is said to be a field." The Sanskrit word for field is *kṣetra*, meaning a plot of farm land. Such land is innocent and pure, for it takes on whatever character the farmer chooses to give it, multiplied many times. A few grains of wheat become a crop. A handful of corn is turned into a harvest.

Land will not resist your intention, for the law of the field seems to be that it will increase whatever you have put into it. You can choose to create a garden that will delight the hearts of all who visit it, or a guest house to provide hospitality for your friends, or a temple where people can come and perform worship. On the other hand, you can turn this same land into a cemetery, or you can use it as a dumping ground for people to come and unload all their garbage. The Lord calls this body a field because you can accomplish in it whatever you choose.

What you sow here and now, you will harvest later. Therefore, sow God in this body by meditating on him.

Swami Muktānanda

Giving is in harmony with God's will.
It is a shining act of love.
Give liberally as God gives.

Swami Muktānanda

When you give what you have to others,
then what you have does not become a
burden for you.

Gurumayi Chidvilāsānanda

*W*hen you do something good for another person,
do it wholeheartedly, expecting nothing in return.

When you give the light of your own heart to
another person, you bring out the best in him;
you give him the power to be what he has the
ability to be.

Gurumayi Chidvilāsānanda

There are all kinds of charitable works, but the greatest charitable act of all is letting a person experience his own divinity.

Gurumayi Chidvilāsānanda

*A*fter God-realization, the results of a realized being's good actions are enjoyed by others. He may distribute sweets or clothes, he may offer *yajñas*, he may go on pilgrimages, or he may perform worship of God — the fruits of all these actions are enjoyed by others.

Those who eat what he gives, those who develop faith in God through him, those who gain knowledge through him — they are the ones who enjoy the fruits of his good actions.

Swami Muktānanda

The Guru's heart is free from passions.
The Guru's heart is immortal.
The Guru's heart is the Absolute.
When, out of compassion,
he bestows grace upon a disciple,
he bestows his own state,
his golden heart, completely.

Gurumayi Chidvilāsānanda

*W*hen we sit for meditation, even though it seems that we're not doing very much, a lot is happening on the inside. This practice is the highest form of *sevā*; it brings about each individual's transformation.

When you carry your inner transformation to wherever you live and wherever you work, you are performing a great service to humanity.

Gurumayi Chidvilāsānanda

Giving is a beautiful path of *dharma*.
For a pure soul, giving is a natural impulse.

Gurumayi Chidvilāsānanda

*B*ecoming unselfish doesn't mean just giving
things to others; it also means keeping yourself
above the fickleness of the mind and perceiving
the Truth at every moment.

Gurumayi Chidvilāsānanda

*E*very desire must become an offering to supreme
Consciousness; then it can be a liberating force in
your life.

As long as you hang on to a desire, it stagnates
in your heart and you have no peace of mind.
However, when you're able to surrender your
desire to the divine Will, it is almost as if you
offer up a piece of glass and receive a jewel in
return. Suddenly you realize, "I am worthy of
God's gift. I *am* worthy of God's gift. I'm *worthy*
of God's gift!" You're able to experience serenity.

Gurumayi Chidvilāsānanda

God is nothing but love
and love is all he gives.

When God is loved,
he becomes totally yours.

Gurumayi Chidvilāsānanda

When you're touched
by God's compassion,
your heart melts with love
and you long to offer yourself
in his service.

Gurumayi Chidvilāsānanda

NOVEMBER

15

*T*he true understanding of *sevā*, selfless service, dawns on a seeker after he receives *śaktipāt*. After receiving grace, you do *sevā* not because anyone needs your services; you serve because your heart is overflowing. Your gratitude takes a form, and it's called *sevā*.

Gurumayi Chidvilāsānanda

In service, the giver and the receiver are connected like two branches growing from the trunk of one tree. Service involves the receiver as much as the giver. The receiver must also perform selfless service.

The receiver must give of himself, returning what he has gained tenfold or a hundredfold. When an exchange like this is in balance, then selfless service actually becomes a sweet dance, a sweet song. You experience the perfection of life. It makes the Lord manifest.

Gurumayi Chidvilāsānanda

*A*lways give freely, withholding nothing.
You will reach God.
A farmer understands the importance of giving.
For the little he gives to the earth,
he receives abundantly in return.

Give freely, as God gives.
If, after giving, you forget about it,
then that gift grows fully.

Swami Muktānanda

It is said that Lakṣmī, the goddess of wealth, loves to live with those people who perform sacred actions through their minds, through their speech, and through their hearts. To such people she reveals the secrets of the universe, and she allows them to experience her in her purity. Those who respect and worship Lakṣmī see her divine glory in everything.

Gurumayi Chidvilāsānanda

*D*on't think about doing something great, wonderful, or splendid. Do something very small. If you see someone who is sad, say something nice. If you see someone in trouble, help him. If you find someone all alone who doesn't know what to do, and then, when you try to help him, he says something unpleasant to you, just listen. Don't say anything back.

Helping someone or performing a good action is very, very subtle. It doesn't just mean doing what everyone else is doing. It also means doing what no one else is doing.

Gurumayi Chidvilāsānanda

*P*erforming a helpful action can also take place within you. When a negative thought arises, be kind to yourself. Instead of putting yourself down, repeat the mantra *Oṁ Namaḥ Śivāya* or think about something that has captured your mind with great love, with deep fascination. Think of the time when you saw a beautiful flower and were amazed that such an exquisite object could be created in this world.

Give to others, be kind to others, and be kind to yourself as well.

Gurumayi Chidvilāsānanda

*G*ive whatever you give with love. Then even
the tiniest pebble you offer will have great meaning.
Its fruit will come back to you a thousandfold,
because it is not the pebble that you give, it is love.

Don't give a gift for the mere sake of the gift;
let there be love in it.

When you give a gift to someone, it's not the object
that really matters; it is the love that goes with it.
That is the true gift, that is the divine exchange.

Gurumayi Chidvilāsānanda

A true devotee completely loses himself in the love of God. He really doesn't care what he receives and what he doesn't receive. His only wish is that the Lord be pleased with him. For such a devotee, nothing exists but the love of God.

When you truly receive God's grace, you want nothing more than his love.

Gurumayi Chidvilāsānanda

*Y*ou can make hundreds of resolutions
each year, yet God has the power to give
you what he believes is good for you.
So the best thing to ask for is patience.
Pray: "O Lord, give me whatever you feel
I'm worthy of, and then give me the patience
and strength to understand your gift and
put it into practice."

You may come up with hundreds of wishes;
nevertheless, if you don't have the patience
to receive God's gift, then everything goes
to waste. Therefore, pray for patience.
Again and again, pray for patience.

Gurumayi Chidvilāsānanda

NOVEMBER

24

It is very important that we live our lives in gratitude toward God and in appreciation for this beautiful life.

Sometimes you feel good. Sometimes you feel bad. Yet there is wonderful ecstasy that's constantly bubbling deep inside each one of us. And this is why we are here: to experience this ecstasy and to give it to other people, also. And then those people can give it to others. In this way we make not just our own life but also the lives of others very beautiful.

Gurumayi Chidvilāsānanda

The glory of giving blessings to others is that the blessings don't go just to one person; they spread like sparks of fire. They touch other beings and other parts of the earth, also.

Gurumayi Chidvilāsānanda

The laws of hospitality are very ancient.
All civilizations recognize that welcoming
strangers as well as friends and family
members is an integral part of what makes
us human. Welcoming is not merely a
polite gesture. It involves accepting the
existence of another person, acknowledging
something beyond our own selfish interests,
acknowledging the One who dwells
within all—the great Lord who abides
in everyone's heart.

Welcoming is the way of the saints. Welcoming
allows other people to recognize their own
goodness, their loveliness, their own innate wisdom.
If you can be generous in welcoming other people,
it does something great for your own heart.

Gurumayi Chidvilāsānanda

The true welcome that goes beyond a person's weaknesses and shortcomings is the natural vision of great beings. They never stop at the level of your mistakes; they look beyond.

When you extend a welcome to someone with genuine feeling, it heightens your own inner state; the return is always much greater than anything you have given.

To see greatness in others and welcome it is one of the most dharmic actions anyone can ever perform.

Gurumayi Chidvilāsānanda

Give yourself to whatever you're doing, so you don't have to worship your ego all the time. Good or bad, however you feel, just give yourself completely.

It's very easy to make excuses, but the best thing you can learn from yoga is to dedicate yourself completely to whatever you choose to do at a particular given moment.

Gurumayi Chidvilāsānanda

*W*hat a seeker wants to do is abandon himself, because it is in self-abandonment that he knows he will find supreme silence and the love of God.

Offer your body to God; let it become the body of God. Offer your mind to God; let it become God's mind. Offer your breath to God; let it be God's breath. In this offering there is great freedom.

Everything that has come from God must return to its source.

Gurumayi Chidvilāsānanda

*W*hen do you receive everything? When you are
totally empty. Simplicity is of the utmost importance.
The moment you are simple, you attain everything.

You cannot bargain with God for love, for devotion, for
a relationship with him. You can only become simple.

Above everything else, be simple. When you are simple,
you merge into God.

Gurumayi Chidvilāsānanda

DECEMBER

The Self Is the Actor

It is said, in the beginning God was alone. But then he had a thought: "Let me become many." Because God could not act out his drama by himself, for his own pleasure he became many, assuming all the strange and unique forms in the universe.

This creation is God's ceaseless play, his unique drama, which he performs for his own amusement. It is an enchanting piece of magic, but it is real.

Swami Muktānanda

_O_ne of the aphorisms in the _Śiva-sūtra_ says:

> _nartaka ātmā_
> _The Self is the actor._

It means that the Self, who can be called the supreme Truth or Consciousness, wears different costumes and appears to change his nature. Assuming different roles, he continues his play in the world.

Where does he play his roles?

Not only is the Self the actor, but the Self is also the stage. He plays different roles upon his own Being. He uses himself as the stage to perform his drama.

Swami Muktānanda

DECEMBER

3

All of us are players on the great stage
of God called the world, and the Self is
the source of all these roles.

Swami Muktānanda

You look up into the night sky and see all the stars and planets hanging in their constellations — each one unique. In the clear, hot air of the desert, you can often see mountains capped with snow sparkling in the distance. Think for a moment of all the different sounds you hear: urban sounds, country sounds, the voice of someone you love, music. Or think of the varieties of bubbles in water — in a mountain stream, in a glass being filled under a faucet, on the crest of an ocean wave. Think of the uniqueness of the in-breath. Think of the uniqueness of the out-breath. Or the wind — even the same wind feels different if you are on a mountaintop or in a valley.

All things appear to exist separately, yet there is an underlying force that sustains each one. And each of us is drawn to them all. This compelling attraction makes you understand that there is a unifying force at work in this cosmos.

Gurumayi Chidvilāsānanda

The unity of the Self is not lost through becoming the universe. Even though it fills the universe, it is not broken up into pieces. The one great Energy has become everything and flows through everyone and everything.

Gurumayi Chidvilāsānanda

The perfect did not change its oneness
even when embodied as the many.
Muktānanda, That is not two.

Understand that the differences
that appear in daily life
are only apparent.
Bracelet, bangle, ring, earring, necklace
are all made of the same gold,
though their appearances differ.

In a blacksmith's workshop,
hammer, tongs, nails, latches, bolts
are made from the same iron.
They are made in different ways
and appear to be different,
but the basic substance is one — iron.

Father, son, mother, Guru, disciple —
all are the manifested compassion
of the compassionate One.
Give up name and form
and you will see what remains —
the unchanging soul.

Swami Muktānanda

DECEMBER

7

*A*ccording to the experience of the saints, even though the Self perceives and becomes countless things and objects, forms and shapes, it is not diminished. It is not depleted. No matter how much you drink from that wellspring, it never loses its fullness.

Gurumayi Chidvilāsānanda

It is true that there are infinite modifications in this
world — birth and death, pain and pleasure, health and
sickness. Some people cry and others laugh. But that
is the nature of the drama. When I was very young,
I saw a play in which a thief killed two people. I cried
bitterly, but the people sitting next to me reassured me
by saying, "Don't worry; it's only a play." That is what
the world is. It is a play of the Lord. The only reason
we experience pain in this world is because we have
not recognized the nature of this play.

Swami Muktānanda

*H*appiness is the twin sister of suffering, and these two
are forever taking turns, paying visits to every living being.
Fortune and misfortune come to call at different times.
Someone whose Śakti has been awakened is able to accept
this without being thrown off course. He or she knows that
all this is a play of Consciousness; so whichever sister comes
to call, such a person thinks, "In the end, this too will lead
me to God's abode."

Gurumayi Chidvilāsānanda

It is God, the Creator, who has made this world a good place to live in by forming the outer world and the inner world in his own image and then pervading both. If God were not in the world, who could live there? Who would strive to make his worldly dealings honest and pure? If the world is interesting and full of joy, it is because of God.

Swami Muktānanda

DECEMBER

11

*W*e find the shadow of God's bliss in the taste of food, in the sweetness of water, in the melodies of *rāgas*, in the soft smile of blossoming flowers, and in the squeals of small children. If God's radiance were not in the beauty of many-colored flowers, why should we be so captivated by them? Why should we love them so? If mangoes, pineapples, tangerines, or pomegranates lacked his beauty, sweetness, and savor, why should they taste so sweet to us? Their sweetness and nectarean savor are due to that divine Principle. There is so much sweetness in plain and pure water! How we love the sun, its bright rays of many colors! At the touch of these delicate rays, lotuses open, plants sway with happiness, the whole kingdom of birds is filled with bliss and begins to sing. Look carefully with subtlety: these sunrays, these creepers, surrender to each other in mutual love and sacrificial worship, and meet each other with silent speech. What divine music there is in the gently blowing wind; what a sweet, cool, happy touch!

All this is the love-flow of God manifest.

Swami Muktānanda

DECEMBER

12

Shaivism says that God has two aspects. He is both transcendent and immanent. In his transcendental aspect he is supremely pure and beyond the world, but in his immanent aspect he is within the world.

True humanity is to see God's divine and unchanging face in his constantly changing drama.

Swami Muktānanda

DECEMBER

13

The Self is transcendent and immanent — beyond the universe, also within the universe. This is why you can worship the form of God and the formlessness of God.

Through the form you reach the formlessness of God. Through something you reach nothing.

Gurumayi Chidvilāsānanda

DECEMBER

14

*E*ndless is the glory,
    endless are the names,
    endless is the sport of the Infinite.

Swami Muktānanda

Most people have the understanding that
Consciousness means something airy and ethereal.
That is the wrong understanding. A brilliant,
orange-colored lizard on the road. The sharp rocks.
The gushing water in the river. The incredible
formation of clouds in the sky. The threat of lightning.
The roaring, raging fire at the bottom of the sea.
Crashing waves. The crumbling earth. Tornado.
Powerful wind. Everywhere you look, the tumultuous
power of Consciousness is raging constantly.

This tumultuous power of Consciousness exists
in the universe, and it exists within every one of us.
Without this vibrating power, there would be
no universe. You yourself would not exist.

Everything is a manifestation of this vibrating,
shimmering power. And this is not just a gentle
shimmering. It is tumultuous.

Every particle of the universe contains the great
power of Consciousness.

Gurumayi Chidvilāsānanda

*Y*ou're sitting quietly: the body is still, the mind has no thoughts, the heart is not murmuring. Everything is very serene. What is roaring inside you? The tumultuous power of Consciousness. How is it roaring? Can you hear its voice? Can you feel its waves? Can you experience the primordial vibration? What is happening? Why does this happen? Even though everyone thinks you are so quiet, you know very well you're not.

Understand the depths of the tumultuous ocean of Consciousness. It is out of this struggle that many poets came into existence, many writers, many wonderful scholars, many artists, great dancers, incredible singers, great thinkers. In some, the tumultuous power of Consciousness takes these forms, and they become the leaders of the world. In others, this same tumultuous power of Consciousness is destructive — these people must struggle just to get a few crumbs of food. The very tumultuous power of Consciousness that gives birth to so much at the same time destroys so much. It is the divine power behind everything.

Gurumayi Chidvilāsānanda

The sages in the past always invoked the grace of the supreme Spirit. These days we feel *we* do everything. In ancient times it was everyone's firm experience that it is the supreme Spirit that makes everyone move, makes everyone think, makes everyone feel, makes everyone act. Therefore, before they performed any action, they always asked for the grace of the supreme Spirit. They prayed, "Come to me, be with me always."

Gurumayi Chidvilāsānanda

I read a story called "The Lord's Club." The club had a rule that only lords were admitted to the premises. But at the first meeting, there was no one to cook, no one to wait on the tables, no one to wash the cups and saucers. There was nobody to do any work because they were all the children of lords. Finally, they wrote down each job on a piece of paper and each lord drew a lot. One of the greatest lords drew the lot that said "guard," so he went to stand at the door. A second one drew the cook's lot, so he went to the kitchen to prepare tea. A third drew his lot and found that he was supposed to wash the plates. A fourth drew the president's lot. A fifth was the secretary. That day their club went very well.

The next time they met, the previous president became the guard. The treasurer became the cook. Because of their destiny they each did their own kind of work. Nonetheless, they were all children of lords and they never lost that feeling.

In the same way, we all do different kinds of work, but none of us has a permanent position. Just as the members of that club always remembered that they were lords, in the same way you should remember that you are the supreme Truth. We are all the children of the Lord.

Swami Muktānanda

*D*o not think, "I am this" or "I am that." These kinds of feelings are transitory. When you are playing a certain role, you have a certain name, but it is not the ultimate Truth.

Swami Muktānanda

*W*hen you turn within and see the Self, you will understand that everything has sprung from the Truth and that therefore everything is the Truth. Then you will understand that you do not have to give up your children, because they will not interfere with your attaining God. You do not have to hate society, because in society too, it is he alone who exists. You do not have to give up your household activities, retreat to a forest, and meditate with your eyes closed. All that you have to do is understand that it is he alone who exists in all your activities and that all the actions you perform are his worship.

If you have this awareness, then your life itself becomes yoga, meditation, and knowledge. If you have this awareness, all knowledge arises from within and you become the embodiment of God.

Swami Muktānanda

DECEMBER

21

$\mathcal{B}$athe in the nectarean knowledge
that the Self and the world are one.

Gurumayi Chidvilāsānanda

DECEMBER

22

In the *Bhagavad-gītā*, Lord Kṛṣṇa says that the same supreme Being stretches in all directions. All activities and pursuits, all names and forms, are only different manifestations of the Truth. Because this is the case, there is no work that is an obstacle on the spiritual path. Anyone who worships God while following his vocation is fulfilling the purpose of his birth. For example, a musician can worship God with music, provided that he has no selfish motive. A teacher can worship God by teaching, provided that he teaches selflessly. A businessman can worship God in his business, provided that he does it without selfish motive. A farmer can worship God by raising crops, provided that he does it selflessly. Doing one's work selflessly means dedicating it to God. No matter what your pursuit in the world, if you dedicate it to God, it becomes a spiritual pursuit.

Swami Muktānanda

*E*very action of our lives touches some chord that vibrates in eternity. It isn't that in this minute you perform a particular action, and then it fades away, forgotten. Whatever action you perform reverberates throughout the cosmos. Whether this action is performed through the body, through the mind, or through your speech, it will sound in eternity.

Everyone's mind is the cosmos, everyone's heart is the cosmos, everyone's being is the universe; so whatever action you perform, good or bad, is going to continue to re-echo. It is never forgotten, nor is it overlooked.

For this reason we must watch our thoughts and actions. When we spend our time very well, the reverberation is also very beautiful. We must be aware of how we are living our lives.

Gurumayi Chidvilāsānanda

*T*hough the Creator does everything,
there is no trace of doership in him.
This is why you can love God unconditionally.

Gurumayi Chidvilāsānanda

DECEMBER

25

It is Christmas Day and the entire world is celebrating. So we, too, will celebrate in our own way. Though not many people saw Christ personally, countless people in the world today remember him, follow his teachings, and consider the day of his birth to be a day of great blessings.

Those who are dear to the Lord, namely, his great devotees, operate on two planes simultaneously. On one plane, they are filled with compassion for suffering people, and they give the message that will deliver them from their suffering. On the other plane, they see the world as nothing but God, and when they see God all around them, they are filled with delight and they begin to dance in ecstasy.

The true concern of a devotee of the Lord is seeing God everywhere, knowing the nature of the Lord, knowing his ways, and experiencing his bliss and his love.

Swami Muktānanda

*W*hen you experience oneness with the great Seer,
the flame merges with the flame, the water merges
with the water, you merge with your own Self.
When this state of the Witness is attained, all the
saṁskāras, all the past impressions, are nothing
more than burned seeds. Then you live freely,
truly independent.

Because of destiny, you may find yourself in a
particular lifestyle, a particular circumstance,
yet within yourself you are a free soul—nothing
binds you at all.

Gurumayi Chidvilāsānanda

*O*nce you see the face of the Truth, even
for a second, you can never forget it. In
that brief moment, the Self fills your heart
with its own essence, which is ambrosia.
It fills your mind with its essence, which
is knowledge, and your understanding of
life is permanently altered.

Even one glimpse of that Reality is enough.

Gurumayi Chidvilāsānanda

*B*ehold the inner Witness, the spectator who watches all the activities of your waking state while remaining apart from them; who dwells in the midst of all action, good or bad, knowing it fully and yet remaining uncontaminated by it; who is that supremely pure, perfect, and ever-unattached Being.

Try to know him who does not sleep during the sleep state, remaining fully aware and witnessing all the events of the dream world. O friends, behold the spectator who remains awake while you sleep, poised far from sleep.

Who is he? He is the pure Witness, the attributeless One. He is the supreme Being. He is within you.

Swami Muktānanda

When you become the Witness, you become
the supreme enjoyer; you observe everything,
but you remain unconcerned.

When you go to a circus, you watch, but
you're not really affected by anything. You
laugh, you weep, you giggle, you chuckle,
you become serious, you howl, and you growl.
But when you go home, you know that all that
was not you; you are separate from it. And this
is why you are able to enjoy it, because you
know you are not this. You are the Witness.

Gurumayi Chidvilāsānanda

If you understand that He is the main actor in this drama of the world, if you understand that He is the great artist, if you understand who He is, then you will know who you are, and you will find sublime peace within.

If you understand His game, you will realize that you and I do not exist; you will realize that only He exists. Then you will understand that you and I are one and the same, and the moment this recognition takes place, love will arise. When you realize this, you will understand the mystery behind my statement, "I welcome you all with all my heart, with great respect and love."

Swami Muktānanda

Only God exists in this world. Therefore, do not give up your family life, do not leave your children, do not spoil your relationship with your husband or wife, do not see faults in your society, and do not beat your head, worrying about the times and death. This world is the strange play of the Lord of all plays, and you have a very small role in his drama. Play it very well, so that everyone can say, "Encore, encore!"

Swami Muktānanda

Guide to Sanskrit Pronunciation

In Sanskrit every letter is pronounced; there are no silent letters. Every letter has only one sound, except for the letter **v** (see below).

LENGTH OF VOWELS

Vowels are either short or long. Short vowels are **a, i, u,** and **ṛ**. Long vowels are **ā, ī, ū, e,** and **o**. A long vowel is held for twice as long as a short one.

VOWELS

The English equivalents are approximations.

a as in *but* or *cup*	**ā** as in *father* or *calm*
i as in *sit* or *pick*	**ī** as in *seat* or *clean*
u as in *put* or *pull*	**ū** as in *pool* or *mood*
e as in *save* or *wait*	**o** as in *coat* or *cone*

ṛ is a vowel pronounced with the tip of the tongue bent slightly back toward the roof of the mouth, while making a sound between the **ur** in *curd* and the **ri** in *cricket*.

The next two vowels are diphthongs, combinations of sounds that are made up of two distinct vowels pronounced in rapid succession. Each diphthong, represented by two letters in English, is written as a single letter in the Sanskrit alphabet and has the same length as a long vowel.

ai is a combination of **a** and **i**, as in *pie* or *sky*.

au is a combination of **a** and **u**, as in *town* or *cow*.

CONSONANTS

c as in *such*, never as in *cave* or *celery*.

ś as in *shine* or *shower*.

CONSONANTS (continued)

ṣ	is pronounced like ś, except that the tip of the tongue is bent slightly back toward the roof of the mouth, as in English *assure*.
t, d, n	are pronounced with the tip of the tongue against the top teeth.
ṭ, ḍ, ṇ	are pronounced with the tip of the tongue bent slightly back to touch the roof of the mouth.
ṁ	denotes not the consonant *m*, but simply a nasalization of the preceding vowel, as in the three nasal sounds in the French phrase *un grand pont*.
ṅ	as in *ink*, *ingot*, or *sing*.
ñ	as in *bench* or *enjoy*.
jñ	as **jny**. Represents a single letter in the Sanskrit alphabet.
r	is a rolled **r**, as in Spanish *para*.
v	is a soft **v** when following a vowel or beginning a word; when following a consonant (as in *tvam*), it is like a **w** but with minimal rounding of the lips.
ḥ	at the end of a line, indicates that the previous vowel is echoed; for example, *śāntiḥ* is pronounced *śāntihi*.

When consonants are followed by **h**, as in **bh**, **ph**, **dh**, or **gh**, the consonant is aspirated, as in *abhor*, *uphold*, *adhere*, or *doghouse*.

A consonant written twice, such as **dd** or **tt**, is pronounced as a single sound and is held twice as long as a single consonant.

Glossary

All non-English terms are Sanskrit unless otherwise indicated.

ABHINAVAGUPTA
A Siddha who was also a philosopher, poet, scholar, prolific author, and one of the central figures of nondual Kashmir Shaivism; his major works were written between 975 and 1025; his best-known disciple was Kṣemarāja. *See also* KASHMIR SHAIVISM; SIDDHA.

ABSOLUTE (Sanskrit = Brahman)
The highest Reality; supreme Consciousness; the pure, untainted, changeless Truth. *See also* CONSCIOUSNESS.

AMṚTĀNUBHAVA
Lit., "nectar of Self-awareness." A lyrical text in poetry on the nature of the supreme Lord, Śiva, and his power of creation, Śakti; written by the great sage Jñāneśvar Mahārāj. *See also* JÑĀNEŚVAR MAHĀRĀJ; ŚAKTI; ŚIVA.

ĀNANDA
Divine bliss; unbounded, transcendent, independent happiness. *See also* SAC-CID-ĀNANDA.

APASMĀRA
Ignorance; the state in which one forgets one's identity with the Divine.

ARJUNA
One of the warrior heroes from the Indian epic *Mahābhārata*; a disciple of Lord Kṛṣṇa. It was to Arjuna that Kṛṣṇa imparted his teachings in the *Bhagavad-gītā*. *See also* BHAGAVAD-GĪTĀ; KṚṢṆA; MAHĀBHĀRATA.

ASHRAM (Hindi = āśram; Sanskrit = āśrama)
A place of disciplined retreat, where seekers engage in spiritual practice and study sacred teachings.

ĀTMAN
See SELF.

AVADHŪT (Hindi; Sanskrit = avadhūta)
An enlightened being who lives in a state beyond body-consciousness and whose behavior is not bound by ordinary social convention.

BĀBĀ (Hindi)

Lit.,"father; grandfather." A term of affection and respect for an elderly person, a saint, or a holy man. Swami Muktānanda was widely known as Bābā.

BHAGAVAD-GĪTĀ

Lit., "song of the Lord." One of the world's treasures of spiritual wisdom, the center-piece of the Indian epic *Mahābhārata*. In its eighteen chapters, Lord Kṛṣṇa instructs his disciple Arjuna about steady wisdom, meditation, the nature of God, the supreme Self, and spiritual knowledge and practice. *See also* KṚṢṆA; MAHĀBHĀRATA; SELF.

BHAGAVĀN

Lit., "the blessed Lord, the blessed one." One who is glorious, illustrious, and venerable. Swami Muktānanda's Guru is known as Bhagavān Nityānanda.

BLUE PEARL (Sanskrit = *nīla-bindu*)

The point of pure Consciousness within each individual that is the core of our true identity and the source of all our powers of perception and action. It is depicted as shining in the space in the crown of the head; a vision of the Blue Pearl is considered to be an auspicious glimpse of the innermost Self. *See also* CONSCIOUSNESS; SELF.

BRAHMAN

See ABSOLUTE.

CHĀNDOGYA UPANIṢAD

One of the longest of the Upaniṣads and source of the teaching *tat tvam asi*, "Thou art That," which is a statement of the identity between oneself and the Absolute. *See also* ABSOLUTE; UPANIṢAD(S).

CIT, CITI, CITI ŚAKTI

The power of universal Consciousness; the creative aspect of God portrayed as the universal Mother, the Goddess. She is known by many names. *See also* CONSCIOUSNESS; KUṆḌALINĪ ŚAKTI.

CITTAṀ MANTRAḤ

Lit., "the mind is mantra." An aphorism from the sacred Indian text *Śiva-sūtra* (2.1). *See also* ŚIVA-SŪTRA(S).

CONSCIOUSNESS (Sanskrit = *cit, citi, saṁvit*)

When capitalized: The luminous, self-aware, and creative Reality that is the essential Self of all that exists; a name for God, the Absolute, the supreme Truth. *See also* SELF.

DARŚAN (Hindi; Sanskrit = *darśana*)

Lit. "seeing, perceiving, knowing." The experience of being in the presence of a holy person. In Siddha Yoga, the inner experience of the Guru's presence; seeing, perceiving, knowing the Guru within; a movement of Śakti within the Heart. *See also* HEART; ŚAKTI; SIDDHA YOGA.

DHARMA

Right action, that which supports and upholds; one's duty, especially the highest spiritual duty; actions that are ultimately beneficial for all; behavior that is in alignment with the cosmic order, with one's religion or spiritual path, and with one's role in life.

DĪKṢĀ

Initiation by a Guru into the spiritual path. In Siddha Yoga, *dīkṣā* takes the form of the awakening of a seeker's Kuṇḍalinī energy by the grace of the Siddha Guru; this initiation is known as *śaktipāt dīkṣā*. *See also* KUṆḌALINĪ ŚAKTI; ŚAKTIPĀT; SIDDHA GURU; SIDDHA YOGA.

EGO (Sanskrit = *ahaṅkāra*, lit., "I-maker")

A faculty of the mind (*antaḥ-karaṇa*) which, in Indian philosophy, constructs one's sense of limited identity, creates the illusion of a separate self with a specific personality and qualities, and appropriates specific objects and experiences to itself. The limitations of the ego can be transcended by engaging in the spiritual practices of *sādhanā*. *See also* SĀDHANĀ.

GURU

Lit., "a venerable person, a spiritual preceptor, a teacher." *When capitalized:* A realized Master, a true Guru. *See also* SIDDHA GURU.

GURU-GĪTĀ

Lit., "song of the Guru." A sacred text consisting of Sanskrit mantras that describe the nature of the Guru, the Guru-disciple relationship, and techniques of meditation on the Guru. Chanting the *Guru-gītā* is one of the central practices of Siddha Yoga students. *See also* GURU; MANTRA; SIDDHA YOGA.

HAṀSA

Lit., "I am (*aham*) That (*saḥ*)." The natural vibration of the Self, which seekers experience within through the Guru's grace, and by which they become aware of their identity with the supreme Self. Also, the mantra formed by the syllables *ham* and *saḥ* (or *so*), repeated with the breath. Also known as the mantra *so'ham*. *See also* MANTRA; SELF.

HEART (Sanskrit = *hṛdaya*)

When capitalized: The supreme Self, the pure Consciousness that is both the divine core of a human being and the essential nature of all things. *See also* CONSCIOUSNESS; HṚDAYA.

HṚDAYA

Lit., "heart." In Sanskrit, the core, that which is essential; also, the physical heart, the psychic instrument, and the individual self. In yogic and philosophical texts, the supreme Self, which pervades each one of us and everything in creation. *See also* SELF.

JAPA

Repetition of a mantra in order to focus the mind and center it in the Heart. On the Siddha Yoga path, one repeats the mantra with the awareness that the mantra, its deity, and its repeater are expressions of one supreme Consciousness. *See also* CONSCIOUSNESS; HEART; MANTRA; SIDDHA YOGA.

JĪVA

The individual identified with the limitations of the mind, the ego, and the senses. *See also* EGO.

JĪVĀTMA

The individual soul; divine Consciousness in an individual. *See also* CONSCIOUSNESS.

JÑĀNEŚVAR MAHĀRĀJ

(1275–1296) The foremost poet-saint of Mahārāṣṭra, also known as Jñānadev. The *Jñāneśvarī*, his commentary in Marathi verse on the *Bhagavad-gītā*, is widely acknowledged as one of the world's greatest spiritual works. *See also* BHAGAVAD-GĪTĀ.

KARMA

Lit., "action." Any action, whether physical, verbal, or mental; also, the fruition of an action arising from desire, whether the effects of such actions are experienced as pleasurable or not pleasurable. The accumulated impressions of karmas shape an individual's past, present, and future life situations.

KASHMIR SHAIVISM

The nondual Shaivism of medieval Kashmir, a philosophy elaborated in the collective writings of a number of sages from Kashmir for whom the name Śiva denoted the ultimate Reality. These sages, who flourished from the ninth through the twelfth centuries, recognized the entire universe as a manifestation of Śiva's Śakti or divine power. Swami Muktānanda found his own experience reflected in the writings of these sages and incorporated many of their core teachings into the philosophical framework of the Siddha Yoga path. *See also* ŚAKTI; SIDDHA YOGA; ŚIVA.

KRṢṆA

Lit., "dark one." The eighth incarnation of Lord Viṣṇu (a name for the all-pervasive, supreme Reality, the sustainer of the universe), called Kṛṣṇa because of the blue-black color of his skin. *See also* BHAGAVAD-GĪTĀ.

KUṆḌALINĪ

See KUṆḌALINĪ ŚAKTI.

KUṆḌALINĪ ŚAKTI

The Goddess Kuṇḍalinī; also, the power of spiritual evolution in a human being. The dormant form of this spiritual energy is represented as lying coiled at the base of the spine (*kuṇḍalinī* means "coiled one"); when awakened and guided by a Siddha Guru and nourished by the seeker's disciplined effort, this energy brings about purification of the seeker's being at all levels, and leads to the permanent experience of one's divine nature. *See also* SIDDHA GURU.

LAKṢMĪ
The goddess who is the embodiment and bestower of prosperity, wealth, good fortune, abundance, success, beauty, grace, charm, splendor, and auspiciousness.

LIBERATION (Sanskrit = *mokṣa*)
Freedom from the cycle of birth and death; the realization of one's own divine Self. *See also* SELF.

MADHYA-DAŚA
Lit., "middle period, middle age, middle state." The still space between the in-breath and the out-breath, which can be used as a point of focus for meditation.

MAHĀBHĀRATA
An epic poem in Sanskrit, attributed to the sage Vyāsa, which recounts the struggle between the Pāṇḍava and Kaurava princes over a disputed kingdom. A vast narrative encompassing a wealth of Indian secular and religious lore, it also contains the spiritual treasure of the *Bhagavad-gītā*. *See also* BHAGAVAD-GĪTĀ.

MAHĀRTHAMAÑJARĪ
Lit., "flower of the Supreme." A short twelfth-century treatise on Kashmir Shaivism by the sage Maheśvarānanda, describing the process of creation, the immanence of God, and the means to attain him. *See also* KASHMIR SHAIVISM.

MANTRA
A sacred invocation; sacred words or divine sounds invested with the power to protect, purify, and transform the awareness of the individual who repeats them. A mantra received from an enlightened Master is enlivened by the power of the Master's attainment.

MASTER
See SIDDHA GURU.

MĀYĀ
The power that veils the true nature of the Self and projects the experience of multiplicity. *See also* SELF.

MUṆḌAKA UPANIṢAD
One of the Upaniṣads, which describes rebirth, liberation, and the role of the Guru on the spiritual path. *See also* GURU; UPANIṢAD(S).

NĪLA-BINDU
See BLUE PEARL.

OṀ
The most sacred of all mantras, the primordial sound of the vibrating cosmos, and an embodiment, in the form of sound, of absolute Consciousness; the pulsation of universal power. *See also* CONSCIOUSNESS; MANTRA.

OM NAMAḤ ŚIVĀYA

The initiation mantra of the Siddha Yoga path, known as the great redeeming mantra for its power to grant both worldly fulfillment and spiritual realization. *Oṁ* is the primordial sound; *namaḥ* is an expression of reverence or honor; *śivāya* denotes "to Śiva" or "to divine Consciousness" (the Lord who dwells within). *See also* CONSCIOUSNESS; MANTRA; OṀ; SIDDHA YOGA; ŚIVA.

PARAMAŚIVA

Lit., "supreme Śiva." The primal Lord; the supreme Guru. *See also* ŚIVA.

PĀRVATĪ

The consort of Lord Śiva; a name of the universal Mother or Śakti. It is Pārvatī who first asks Lord Śiva to explain how a seeker can attain union with him; her question and his reply form the text of the *Guru-gītā*. *See also* GURU-GĪTĀ; ŚAKTI; ŚIVA.

PRASĀD (Hindi; Sanskrit = *prasāda*)

Lit., "grace." A blessed or divine gift from God or the Guru.

PRATYABHIJÑĀ-HṚDAYAM

Lit., "the heart of recognition." An eleventh-century treatise by Kṣemarāja that expounds on the *pratyabhijñā* (recognition) philosophy of Kashmir Shaivism. It teaches that individuals, having forgotten their true nature, can once again recognize their own Self through divine grace and an experiential understanding of supreme Consciousness as the essence of all creation. *See also* CONSCIOUSNESS; KASHMIR SHAIVISM; SELF.

PŪRṆO'HAṀ-VIMARŚA

Lit., "I am perfect (*pūrṇo'ham*) awareness (*vimarśa*)." The awareness, "I am complete, full, and perfect."

RĀGA

A melodic form used in classical Indian music. The *rāgas* evoke particular moods in the listener and are often performed to resonate with a season or time of day.

RĀMA (Hindi = Rām)

A name for God. Also, the legendary hero who was the seventh incarnation of Viṣṇu (a name for the all-pervasive, supreme Reality, the sustainer of the universe), the central character in the Indian epic *Rāmāyaṇa*, and an exemplar of *dharma*, or righteousness. *See also* DHARMA.

SAC-CID-ĀNANDA

Lit., "existence, consciousness, and bliss." The three indivisible attributes used in Vedantic philosophy to describe the Absolute. *See also* ABSOLUTE; CONSCIOUSNESS.

SADGURU

A true Guru.

SĀDHAKA

Lit., "one who is accomplishing, fulfilling, or perfecting." A spiritual practitioner who has taken up a specific *sādhanā* or set of spiritual practices taught by a specific lineage of Masters. *See also* SĀDHANĀ.

SĀDHANĀ

Leading straight to a goal; a means of accomplishing (something); spiritual practice; worship. The *sādhanā* of Siddha Yoga students, which begins with *śaktipāt* initiation, includes active, disciplined engagement with the essential Siddha Yoga practices of meditation, chanting, *sevā*, and *dakṣiṇā* (offering of financial resources), along with focused study and contemplation of the Siddha Yoga teachings. The goal of Siddha Yoga *sādhanā* is the spiritual transformation that leads to liberation. *See also* LIBERATION; ŚAKTIPĀT; SEVĀ; SIDDHA YOGA.

SAHASRĀRA

Lit., "one thousand spokes." The highest spiritual center of the subtle body and the destination of the awakened Kuṇḍalinī; located at the crown of the head, it is often visualized or represented as a lotus with one thousand petals. *See also* KUṆḌALINĪ ŚAKTI; SUBTLE BODY.

ŚAKTI

Power, energy, strength. Also, a specific power or energy, such as a power embodied in a particular goddess or within an aspirant. *When capitalized:* The creative power of the divine Absolute, which animates and sustains all forms of creation; often personified as the Goddess, and sometimes more specifically as Kuṇḍalinī Śakti, the power of spiritual evolution in a human being. *See also* ABSOLUTE; KUṆḌALINĪ ŚAKTI.

ŚAKTIPĀT (Hindi; Sanskrit = *śakti-pāta*)

Lit., "descent of power; descent of grace." In Siddha Yoga, the initiation (*dīkṣā*) by which a Siddha Guru transmits the divine grace that awakens Kuṇḍalinī Śakti, the inner spiritual energy in an aspirant; *śaktipāt dīkṣā* signals the beginning of Siddha Yoga *sādhanā*, which culminates in spiritual liberation. *See also* KUṆḌALINĪ ŚAKTI; LIBERATION; SĀDHANĀ; SIDDHA GURU; SIDDHA YOGA.

SAMĀDHI

The practice of absorption in the object of meditation. Also, the final stage of that practice, in which the meditator is absorbed in the Self. *See also* SELF.

ŚĀMBHAVĪ MUDRĀ

A state of spontaneous or effortless absorption in which the eyes are open while the gaze is deep within, breathing is suspended, and the mind delights in the inner Self without any attempt at concentration. *See also* SELF.

SAMSKĀRA

An impression left on the subtle body by past actions or experiences. The set of one's *samskāras* influences how one experiences and reacts to the world in the present. *See also* SUBTLE BODY.

SAT

See TRUTH.

SELF (Sanskrit = *ātman*)

When capitalized: The pure Consciousness that is both the divine core of a human being and the essential nature of all things. *See also* CONSCIOUSNESS.

SELF-REALIZATION

See LIBERATION; SELF.

SEVĀ

Lit., "service; honoring; worship." In Siddha Yoga contexts, selfless service: work offered to God and the Guru, performed as a pure offering, without attachment to the results of one's actions and without desire for personal gain. *See also* SIDDHA YOGA.

SHAIVISM

The Indian religious and philosophical traditions that use the name Śiva to denote the ultimate Reality. In Siddha Yoga, the term *Shaivism* is generally used to refer to the nondual Shaivism of Kashmir. *See also* KASHMIR SHAIVISM; SIDDHA YOGA; ŚIVA.

SIDDHA

A perfected, fully accomplished, Self-realized yogi; an enlightened yogi who lives in the state of unity consciousness; one whose experience of the Self is uninterrupted and whose identification with the ego has been dissolved. *See also* EGO; SELF; YOGI.

SIDDHA GURU

A perfected spiritual Master who has realized his or her oneness with God, and who is able both to bestow *śaktipāt* initiation and to guide seekers to spiritual liberation. Such a Guru is also required to be learned in the scriptures and to belong to a lineage of Masters. *See also* LIBERATION; ŚAKTIPĀT; SIDDHA.

SIDDHA YOGA

The spiritual path taught by Gurumayi Chidvilāsānanda and her Guru, Swami Muktānanda. The journey of the Siddha Yoga path begins with *śaktipāt dīkṣā* (spiritual initiation). Through the grace of the Siddha Yoga Master and the student's own steady, disciplined effort, the journey culminates in the constant recognition of divinity within oneself and within the world. *See also* ŚAKTIPĀT.

ŚIVA

Lit., "auspicious." In nondual Shaivism, the transcendent, immanent, and all-pervasive Reality, the one source of all existence. Also, absolute Reality personified as the supreme Deity, Lord Śiva. *See also* KASHMIR SHAIVISM.

ŚIVA-SŪTRA(S)

An important text in the tradition of nondual Shaivism, said to have been revealed to the sage Vasugupta in Kashmir around the middle of the ninth century. The text consists of seventy-seven aphorisms (*sūtras*) conveying profound teachings on the nature of Reality. *See also* KASHMIR SHAIVISM; ŚIVA.

ŚRĪ

Lit., "auspiciousness." A term of respect that connotes auspicious attributes such as abundance, beauty, nobility, sacredness, and good fortune.

SUBTLE BODY (Sanskrit = *sūkṣma-śarīra*)

The body that is composed of a subtle form of *prāṇa* (vital energy), considered in traditional Indian philosophy to be distinct from the gross or physical body; and which contains the system of energy centers and channels through which Kuṇḍalinī Śakti moves. *See also* KUṆḌALINĪ ŚAKTI.

SUNDARDĀS

(ca. 1596–1689) A poet-saint of Delhi, India, who wrote eloquently about the significance of the spiritual Master and the requirements of discipleship.

SŪTRA

Lit., "thread." An aphorism or concise teaching, intended to be understood with the aid of a commentary, and whose artful brevity supports its memorization.

SVADHARMA

The natural or highest duty of each human being, which is to recognize one's own inner divinity. *See also* DHARMA.

SVĀDHYĀYA

The regular, disciplined practice of chanting and recitation of sacred texts in Sanskrit; also, the process of gaining insight into the nature of the Self through this practice. *See also* SELF.

ŚVETĀŚVATARA UPANIṢAD

One of the principal Upaniṣads, consisting of 113 verses, in which the sage Śvetāśvatara speaks of Brahman, the Absolute, in its manifest aspect. *See also* UPANIṢAD(S).

SWAMI

A monk in an Indian monastic order. Some swamis are teachers. The ten monastic orders to which most of the swamis of India belong were founded by the sage Śaṅkarācārya in the eighth century.

TAPASYĀ (Hindi; Sanskrit = *tapas*)

Lit., "heating." Yogic austerities and disciplined practice (which generate inner heat or "yogic fire") performed to purify both mind and body of any residue of past experience that obscures the direct experience of God; any focused effort in *sādhanā*. *See also* SĀDHANĀ; YOGA.

THAT (Sanskrit = *tat*)

When capitalized: The supreme Self, the Absolute. *See also* ABSOLUTE; SELF.

THREE WORLDS

Heaven, earth, and the netherworld.

TRUTH (Sanskrit = *sat, satya, tattva, paramārtha*)

When capitalized: The highest Reality.

TWO-PETALED LOTUS

The *ājñā-cakra*; the spiritual center in the subtle body located between the eyebrows. This *cakra*, when seen in meditation, appears to be in the form of a lotus with two petals. It is said that the awakened Kuṇḍalinī Śakti passes through this *cakra* only at the command (*ājñā*) of the inner Guru. *See also* KUṆḌALINĪ ŚAKTI; SUBTLE BODY.

UPANIṢAD(S)

Lit., "the sitting down near (a teacher)" or "secret doctrine." The group of scriptures that distill the esoteric teachings of the Vedas and are the basis for Vedantic philosophy. Most of the various Upaniṣads illuminate the essential teaching that the individual soul and the Absolute are one. *See also* ABSOLUTE; VEDA(S).

VASIṢṬHA

The legendary sage and Guru of Lord Rāma, who, in the *Yoga-vāsiṣṭha* scripture, answers Lord Rāma's questions on the nature of life, death, and human suffering by teaching that the world is as you see it and that illusion ceases when the mind is stilled. *See also* RĀMA.

VEDA(S)

Lit., "knowledge." The earliest scriptural compositions of ancient India, regarded as divinely revealed, eternal wisdom. The four Vedas are, in order of antiquity, the *Ṛg-veda* ("Knowledge of the Hymns"), the *Yajur-veda* ("Knowledge of the Sacrificial Formulas"), the *Sāma-veda* ("Knowledge of the Songs of Praise"), and the *Atharva-veda* ("The Knowledge of [Sage] Atharvan").

VIVEKA-CŪḌĀMAṆI

Lit., "the crest jewel of discrimination." A Sanskrit commentary by the eighth-century sage Śaṅkarācārya on Advaita (nondual) Vedānta, expounding the teaching that the Absolute alone is real. *See also* ABSOLUTE.

WITNESS

When capitalized: The transcendental Consciousness that lies at the root of the mind and from which the mind can be observed. *See also* CONSCIOUSNESS; SELF.

YAJÑA

An ancient fire ritual in which oblations are offered to the fire while sacred mantras are chanted to honor the divine powers of the universe. *See also* MANTRA.

YOGA

Lit., "yoking; joining." A method or set of disciplined spiritual practices (including meditation, mantra repetition, concentration, posture, sense control, and ethical precepts) whose ultimate goal is the constant experience of union with the divine Self. *See also* MANTRA; SELF.

YOGI (masc.; *yoginī* = fem.)

One who practices yoga. *See also* YOGA.

Further Reading

PUBLISHED BY THE SYDA FOUNDATION

Selected Books by
Gurumayi Chidvilāsānanda

COURAGE AND CONTENTMENT

Opening with Gurumayi's Siddha Yoga Message talk for 1997, *Wake Up to Your Inner Courage and Become Steeped in Divine Contentment*, this volume includes eight talks in which Gurumayi unfolds the subtle connections between courage and contentment. To face life's challenges with courage and yet to feel content no matter what happens—this is the fruit of ongoing spiritual practice. It is a fruit, Gurumayi teaches, that ripens with intention, constancy, and patience.

ENTHUSIASM

This volume includes talks Gurumayi gave on the Siddha Yoga Message for 1996, *Be Filled with Enthusiasm and Sing God's Glory*. "Seize the opportunity to discover boundless enthusiasm," Gurumayi tells us. "Let the practices of yoga unfold miraculous experiences for you." Gurumayi explores virtues such as patience, forgiveness, gentleness, service, and gratitude—all of which enable us to cultivate our innate enthusiasm and ultimately to perceive God's glory everywhere in every moment of our lives.

INNER TREASURES

The treasures of joy, peace, and love, Gurumayi tells us, are not outer experiences that may be won or lost. They are qualities of our inner being that can be cultivated through spiritual discipline. Turning toward the Heart again and again is the key to making joy, peace, and love an everyday reality.

THE MAGIC OF THE HEART
Reflections on Divine Love

"In the supreme Heart the Lord reveals himself every second of the day." By contemplating Gurumayi's poetic reflections on divine love, we gain insights into how we can come to live in this experience.

MY LORD LOVES A PURE HEART
The Yoga of Divine Virtues

In a series of commentaries on chapter 16 of the *Bhagavad-gītā*, Gurumayi offers precise guidance on how to manifest the magnificent virtues of fearlessness, purity of being, steadfastness, freedom from anger, respect, compassion, humility, and selfless service.

REMEMBRANCE

In *Remembrance*, Gurumayi teaches the practice of acknowledging our own virtues. By remembering our innate goodness, our worthiness to give and receive love, and the extraordinary blessings that flow through our lives, we uplift ourselves and, with renewed conviction, contribute our best to the world.

SĀDHANĀ OF THE HEART
Siddha Yoga Messages for the Year

Each talk in this collection was originally presented to Siddha Yoga students as a message for the year, and each one endures as a focus of contemplation and a source of revelation. These talks, shining with Gurumayi's wisdom and practical guidance, support a seeker's effort on the journey to the experience of the supreme Heart.

THE YOGA OF DISCIPLINE

By contemplating the talks in this volume, the reader learns how to cultivate yogic discipline and how to apply it to everyday activities. Chapters include Gurumayi's discussions on how to bring yogic discipline to seeing, listening, eating, speaking, and thinking, so that we can "break through boundaries and reach the highest goal."

MEDITATE
Happiness Lies Within You

Speaking about the practice of Siddha Yoga meditation, Swami Muktānanda encourages us to turn our attention within and discover the radiant inner world. Bābā gives clear and authoritative answers to such timeless questions as: Who am I, really? How can I master my mind? What is the value of meditation? "The best object of meditation is the inner Self," Bābā tells us. "When the Self is the goal of meditation, why should we choose another object? If we want to experience the Self, we should meditate on the Self."

MUKTESHWARI

These autobiographical verses are among Swami Muktānanda's earliest writings. In studying them, the reader engages with the mystical and practical subtleties of Siddha Yoga *sādhanā*.

PLAY OF CONSCIOUSNESS
A Spiritual Autobiography

This unique spiritual autobiography describes Swami Muktānanda's own process of inner transformation under the guidance of his Guru, Bhagavān Nityānanda. A rare opportunity to study the first-hand account of a Siddha Master's journey to Self-realization.

WHERE ARE YOU GOING?
A Guide to the Spiritual Journey

A lively anecdotal introduction to the teachings of the Siddha Yoga path, this book draws from talks given by Swami Muktānanda in public programs in many different places and times. Answering the question that Bābā chose for the title of this book stirs profound contemplation: "Where *am* I going? What *am* I really doing with my life?" This compendium of Bābā's teachings covers the stages of the spiritual journey from the first understanding of its purpose to the achievement of its goal: perfect freedom and joy.

To learn more about
the Siddha Yoga teachings and practices,
visit the Siddha Yoga path website at:

www.siddhayoga.org

ༀ

For further information about
SYDA Foundation books
and audio, video, and DVD recordings,
visit the Siddha Yoga Bookstore website at:

www.siddhayogabookstore.org

or call 845-434-2000, extension 1700.

From the United States and Canada,
call toll-free 888-422-3334.